"PEACE" AN EXPRESSION OF MENTAL ILLNESS

"PEACE" AN EXPRESSION OF MENTAL ILLNESS

Luanie Lion BlessUp Lambey-Bermudez

Independently Published

LAS VEGAS

CONTENTS

DEDICATION N SPECIAL THANKS

LUANIE LION BLESSUP LAMBEY-BERMUDEZ

"PEACE" IS DEDICATED TO THE GARIFUNA TRIBE N THE VILLAGE THAT RAISED ME.

IF YOU DO SOMETHING EVERYDAY EVENTUALLY, YOU WILL MASTER IT, TO INCLUDE YOURSELF.

SPECIAL THANKS

TO

MY GOD, MY ANCESTORS, CELESTINE DIEGO, STICKY SWEET, MISTAH KYNG, NUNU, VAY, SMUSH, NYNY, DEEN BEAN, JUNJUN, QUEENS, PAW PAW, BONES, SPECIAL, MY-YO, MB, FRANKIE BAY-B, KYNG GIFTED, AIM DANGRIGA, MIL-TONY, BIG KEV, WAH-MOO, CALIYON$UPREME, HARDY BEANZ, REP. JR, KASHA KAINE, NIK-KEY BEANZ, AND THE KINGZ OF MY YOUTH.

ALL MY BREAD-AHS' SLEEPING IN THE STREETS, IN JAILS, PRISONS, LOONEY BINS, HAVING A HARD TIME, AND/OR OPPRESSED KEEP YOUR FAITH.

ABOUT THE AUTHOR

Luanie Lion BlessUp Lambey-Bermudez

I am a father of six children (maybe 7, I

have a loose Cock), a husband to a loving, intelligent, beautiful wife. I am a poet at heart who uses different mediums to express that poetry. Twelve years of military service has left me with scars that can and cannot be seen. After a severe mental break, homelessness, and years of being in the care of the VA, I was finally able to get back on my feet. I now live on the Left Coast in Sizzle Town. I am a creator of conversation and promoter of personal growth. Over 10 years as an established poet, writer, serial-expressionist, and magazine editor. I completed bachelor's degree at University of Central Florida and currently enrolled in a master's program at University of Nevada, Las Vegas. BlessUp

INTRO: PEACE

LUANIE LION BLESSUP LAMBEY-BERMUDEZ

PEACE and blessings reader, welcome to my EXPRESSION OF MENTAL ILLNESS, 2017 was the first glimpse into that expression. PEACE: AN EXPRESSION OF MENTAL ILLNESS is broken down into signs and symptoms and placed into fitting categories; PTSD, BIPOLAR, HYPERMANIA, MEDICATED, and PEACE. Each category represents a reoccurring cycle of mental illness and the struggle for management within that moment. PEACE:

AN EXPRESSION OF MENTAL ILL-NESS is organized in order with my recovery and should be read as such. Without that lens, I fear the reader will be lost in the wild structure rather than in the management of my mental illness. This is a long poem of PEACE, how much PEACE means to me, and what it takes every day to obtain/maintain PEACE. This ain't no fucking game. Every day I wake up pissed off at the world. I have to go through a process of each category just to function as a member of our society. PEACE: AN EXPRESSION OF MENTAL ILLNESS has held off two suicides already, I know it will help hold off countless others. Enjoy and BlessUp, Lion

ABOUT THE AUTHOR

Luanie   Lion   BlessUp   Lambey-
Bermudez

I am a father of six children (maybe 7, I

have a loose Cock), a husband to a loving, intelligent, beautiful wife. I am a poet at heart who uses different mediums to express that poetry. Twelve years of military service has left me with scars that can and cannot be seen. After a severe mental break, homelessness, and years of being in the care of the VA, I was finally able to get back on my feet. I now live on the Left Coast in Sizzle Town. I am a creator of conversation and promoter of personal growth. Over 10 years as an established poet, writer, serial-expressionist, and magazine editor. I completed bachelor's degree at University of Central Florida and currently enrolled in a master's program at University of Nevada, Las Vegas. BlessUp

DISCLAIMER

"PEACE" AN EXPRESSION OF MEN-
TAL ILLNESS

is a work of creative non-fiction. Even though, the events laid out are true to the best of my recollection. The names have been made up and do not exist. The things described in this book can be triggering and harmful to an unhealed mind. Please if you are experiencing abuse or suicidal thoughts, please web search the proper hotline. If you are a veteran reach to the hotline at 988 or text 838255. If nothing else,

reach out to me at 3218059411.
BlessUp

Chapter 1

POST-TRAUMATIC SYNDROME DISORDER

LUANIE LION BLESSUP LAMBEY-BERMUDEZ

WAR STORY

IS THIS WHAT THE FEAR

IS ALL ABOUT, MY BATTLE SAID, NIGGA,

I CAN DO EIGHT MONTHS OUT HERE

IRAQIS DON'T CARE. AS HE PUSHES

THE WOODEN DOOR FOREWARD

N STEPS OUTSIDE, BOOM!!

I DIVE BACK INTO THE HALLWAY

HOPIN' THAT MY BATTLE WOULD LIVE

TO SEE ANOTHER DAY. BOOM!! SHIT,

LORD YOU CAN'T LET THIS HAPPEN.

JUS YESTERDAY, WIT MY SON,

I PLAYED, WIT MY WIFE I

LAYED. IN IRAQ NOT EVEN 24HRS

N I'M FINNA BE SLAYED. REFLECT

ON   MISTAKES   N
THINGS I'VE DONE

WRONG. AHH

(I)   BREATH...   WHAT
THE FUCK,

THIS   SHIT   HURT!
PIECES OF THE DOOR

BEFRIENDING   MY
TIBIA, BROUGHT ME
BACK

2 REALITY. (I) DIDN'T CRY

OR BECOME SAD, I FELT MYSELF GETTING' MAD

THERE'S NO WAY MY YOUTH'S GROWING

UP WITHOUT DAD. GET THE FUCK

UP BLESSUP, GRAB YO VEST N YO HELMET,

PUT A ROUND IN THE
SHOT-EE. U GOT ONE

IN YO LEG, MAKE UMM
FEEL

IT IN THEY BOTTY.
SIRENS AND BULLETS

IS ALL I CAN HEAR.
LOOK DOWN AND I

SEE THE BLOWN OFF
ARMS OF ONE

OF   MY   PEERS.
KNUCKLE UP NIGGA,

SWALLOW YO FEARS,
PULL YO SHIT

AND USE IT. THERE'S
ONE

OVER THERE, BOOM!!
CLICK CLICK

BOOM, CLICK CLICK
BOOM, CLICK CLICK...

I WALK UP ON THE LIFE LESS CADAVER

LYING   THERE TWISTED UP ON THE GROUND,

LOOKED   INTO   HIS SHOT GUNNED FACE

DU WAS DARK LIKE ME, I ALMOST BROKE

DOWN. THIS IS ONE OF MANY REASONS

WHY AT NIGHT I DON'T SLEEP. WHEN I

CLOSE MY EYES THE SAME NIGHTMARE

I DREAM. THE SAME SHOT GUNNED FACE

I SEE.

JULY

I have gotten everything I ask(ed) for, I continue to shine in this realm, I am seeing people watching me, I made mention bout being recorded and the room went silent. I keep putting myself in situations to experience new things, I'm pushing the envelope in this reality, I am seeing that I truly have no limits, Thanks for listening.

THE THANKS FOR MY SERVICE

A jailhouse spoken word

"The Beloved has always had a hand on my life."

LionBlessUp

Hands on the steering wheel

the driver's head is against the driver's

side window, I'm driving from the back

seat, swerving. This nigga's screaming

for help, this is all his fault, All I

asked was, "How did he find me".

On the left of us, is a red ford focus

the driver was Tyrion Lannister

sending me mental messages,

"Do something before they kill you" .

I send a message back , "I'm on it, they will never

accomplish that". I turn the wheel left

purposely hitting the focus on its passenger

side, Tyrion and I kept eye contact I wondered

which one of us was going to win the staring contest

the driver yanked the steering wheel right,

we came to a stop, he hopped out like an athlete

bursting through a paper sign, I followed suit

and popped out too. The driver had his hands high

above his head, they were flailing

like a tube men sign "Ahh help me,

help me, he's crazy". I gave chase, I had questions

and he had the answers, when I looked up I

saw the jakes, I ran back to the taxi

I looked over at the passenger seat

and grabbed his black Jan Sport, dumped

all the contents out, I saw my L's and my social

security card, Both things mysteriously disappeared

from inside my girls Toyota Corolla a month ago.

I looked through the back window and saw the police

getting closer, I put the car in drive and promised

myself to get back at all the cowards

that was down with this. I pulled off the wall and shot

into the middle lane, the car was driving weird,

like a big wheel when the handlebars was inverted.

The police were gaining on me so I

turned into a white compact vehicle,

hoping it would slow down my pursuers.

Unfortunately, the taxi's fender got smacked

and the cab twirled back into the wall, Adrenaline

allowed me to shake it off and check for my predators,

I spot one patty wagon, four marked, and three

unmarked vehicles lined up five abreast

moving in unison like a police call before the range

gets inspected. I start pushing the gas,

both front tires are spinning but the cab

isn't progressing, No problem I can run
all day.

Look down at my high-top basketball
shoes

and say a prayer "BELOVED protect me
I'm on foot".

I take off across the highway, juking and
strafing

like a linebacker in *Madden*, I made it to
the middle

of the highway hopped up on the shoulder

pressed myself on top the concrete
median,

I start tight roping it, walking across

the top of the median in a quarter bend
stance.

I see the exit for the international'

airport off to the right, that's where I'm
headed,

some white guy in a white two door
truck

early two thousand types, pulls up right
beside me,

I remember looking down and saying,
whoa,

whoa, almost falling from a break in
concentration,

the guy says, "What are you doing?

You're going to have to stop running

sooner or later. You should just hop down and face

this, men", then disappears down the highway, I

jumped down, ran across the cleared highway

looking at about five cop cars, two patty wagons,

a couple of sport utility vehicles. Making my way

to the exit, a cop I have met before runs

in front of me, stops, squares up with me

then pulls a black Beretta military issue,

aims it so I can see the darkness in the barrel

then the cop says "Luanie,

I'm only going to say this one time. Get on your fucking

knees" the cop takes three deep breaths, takes two

full steps forward, positioning the weapon right

between my eyes, the barrel was no longer visible

to me. "Place your hands behind your head, do it,

and do it NOW. I looked the cop in his eyes, I

thought of how his pupils resemble the barrel

of his weapon. Here's my chance to die

without doing myself, suicide by cop.

In that same instant, I realized I wanted to live

and got on my fucking knees and put my hands

behind my head.

PART TWO

While being subdued by the police, I realized most of them, I had served (military) with them in some capacity or another. They greeted me by my name and told me to sit back, everything was going to be ok now that they were here, I will be good 2 go. I yelled, "I'm sorry" out the window, a cop I remembered from Afghanistan (black big built brother), he shook his head and waved me off with a light fly swat. Behind the squad car by the left side of the trunk, eight to nine cops discuss the next step. I sat back smiling and happy to be rescued by familiar faces. Two cops got in the front seats. I'm sitting behind the driver with my knees turn to the right side off my body. I have balance thanks to the meat on my left thigh taking the brunt of the pressure off my tailbone and the handcuffs keep my shoulders pinched. I say, "Thank God you'll came and got me, they were tryna…" "Shh" one of the officers said cutting me off, "Shh, they can hear you", pointing to the radio. I nod north and south, lay back and started singing a popular 90's rock song by some white guy who paints his face white with black make-up rounding out his eyes "I would do anything for love, but I won't do that". We pulled up to some abandoned warehouses protected by a gated fence with curly Constantine wire connected at the top. The driver waved a badge in front of some type of a sensor, the gate took it's time opening, we drove in and headed towards the loading dock of what seemed to be the biggest warehouse there. We pull up the driver gets out the car first his partner followed but before he exited turns to me and instructs me to stay put. They disappear into the warehouse without a trace. I don't know how long they were gone but when they returned to the car, they seemed refocused, on what I had no clue. In my mind, I had just been rescued by my military brothers and was about to be taken some where safe to debrief. What I had to debrief is still a mystery in my mind. So with that belief, I laid my head back against the uncomfortable plastic sit, closed my eyes. my door opened and my eyes opened when I felt medium sized hands firmly cup my biceps guiding me out the car. I remember getting out without my shoes on, just my socks. The cop asked where my shoes were and I said in the back seat, I didn't need them to debrief. The cop told me to put them on I will be needed them soon again.

Finally, I looked around to my surroundings. I was confused at the sight of other cop cars, a concrete building with big windows, through the windows are people. Some were sitting with their heads down, some was walking back and forth, some was standing against the glass like a car sticker. Why are we here? I asked hoping the answer would calm my anxieties about why the fuck they brought me to a jail. The answer was simple and sounded dry "This is the safest place for you, we will be back for you after we conduct our interrogations". I obliged with the officers and followed them through the double set of steel doors, I was put into a cell with one aluminum toilet and a concrete bed protruding the back wall. Before the doors shut one of the cops turned to me made eye contact with me and said, "You did good Luanie, really good, see you soon".

The door shut in front of me and I remember feeling relieved and special.

PART THREE

The door to my cell slid left;

eight cops entered

some with pepper spray

and others with a stun gun.

I stood up from the concrete bed

doing my best follow the commands

being shouted my way,

a cop who I know is the Iron Sheikh

from nineties wrestling puts his stun gun to face,

I had to turn around N face the wall,

I was allowing my tears to fall,

I knew one move outside of the many commands

would start my beatdown,

I was instructed to remove my clothing, drop

them to the floor and kick them behind me

shortly after compliance, I felt a gloved hand molest

every part of my body starting from my ankles up to shoulders,

I bent over and opened my ass

for them to check inside I turned around lifted up my dick

then my balls, I squatted down and coughed, the eight cops

exited my holding cell tactically, it resembled a Roman

infantry formation, I watched them leave

and knew they would be back for the fight

that they were promised. A pair of blue coveralls

was left on my concrete bed. A pair of brown

slides was also waiting for my feet.

I got dressed and sat on the raised concrete

bed. The Iron Sheikh came to my cell

looking through the little square (window), I looked in his eyes

and he mouthed "We are going to kill

you", then walks away. I immediately
went into action;

First, I forced out an arm length doo doo
log

in the aluminum toilet/sink combina-
tion,

Second, I took pieces of the log out

of the toilet bowl, smeared it

all on the inside of my blue coveralls,

then I did the same for the outside of the coveralls,

I think of it as added make up foundation before the beatdown,

Third, I took more pieces from the log and painted

the walls as thick as I can, starting from the doors

including the little ass window, moving clockwise applying boo

boo until my cell looked like the inside of a brown moving box,

Lastly was my feet, arms, hands, and face, I rub that shit

on my skin like fresh coconut oil, taking
my time

to make sure to cover all exposed areas.

I was sitting for about thirty minutes

(I really don't freaking recall) when the
door

to my cell slid open, the cops in their
Charlie's

Angel's formation, took one step forward

and the first one in, shook his head,
dropped

his shoulders N started clutching his
stomach.

They backed out fast and in step

(They legs look like one of the green dudes

from a famous Halloween special), I think they decided killing

me can wait for a while, I smiled,

laid my head against the back wall, exhaled, closed

my eyes, and let my soul have a discussion

with the almighty.

"On your feet Sarnt (Sergeant)"

I lift my lids, two chevrons appeared at the dookie

encrusted window, "On your feet Sarnt",

I pop tall and get at attention;

Feet forty-five-degree angle

knees slightly bent so I

won't pass out, hands curled tight

like I'm holding a roll of quarters,

thumbs aligned with the imaginary

seam of my coveralls, back erected,

shoulders rolled back, chest out,

head up, and chin down,

mouth twist up with my bottom

lip showing off an imaginary tattoo,

looking through the Sergeant, I'm locked and cocked.

I don't remember the sergeants' features,

only his body blur and chevrons,

I know he was about seventy-one inches

tall slender with a bold cut or little blonde

curls either way, I did as commanded,

"Listen soldier, I am going to open your cell

I need you to walk directly out and stay behind me."

"Yes Sergeant, roger THAT", strong and loud was my response.

I followed the Sergeant into a room that was mostly glass

with metal trimmings. He opened a metal

door for me, I entered without hesitation. I

heard the lock to the door click behind me.

"Soldier you are going to remove your coveralls

and push them out the slot in front of you,

do you understand?" "Roger", I responded. Removed

my crusting dookie suit (protective cloak)

and hurried it out the slot. A gloved hand

slid the coveralls into a bag (black) then puts a white

bar soap on the slot door. "Soldier shower

and use the soap I provided you with",

"Roger, sergeant" my response.

I remember rubbing the bar up and down

my shins talking with the Sergeant,

about what, I haven't a clue. I told one of the corrections

officer, he looked the wrestler from Iran,

the sergeant and I had a good laugh. The corrections

officer looked me my eyes, all I had seen in his iris

was flames. I did my best to pay

attention to the exits, the procedures for opening

doors, and if anyone knew me or resembled

someone I served with in the Army,

we walked into a Lear that had the lights

dimmed with about five cells, each cell

carved into a stone wall,

plexiglass surrounded the metal door.

To the right was a long desk (brown or black)

littered with paper and fast-food bags,

two desktops and two corrections officers

sitting in thin office chairs. The two officers

were watching a singing competition

on the desktop (maybe) and paid no attention

to us walking toward them. "Gentlemen,

we need a cell", the sergeant's voice had no

candy in it. Both officers stood up

and got moving, one started shuffling

papers on the desk, the other walked

us down to the last of the five cells.

I'm busy paying attention to the back exit,

to notice walking into my new cell. While taking note

of my surroundings, I overhear the back and forth

between the sergeant and the two offi-cers

"Who is he?" One officer asks. "I don't care who he is,

just use these numbers as his identifier". "Sergeant

that makes no sense, how long are we keeping him?"

"We do not pay you to make sense of things, I

haven't any knowledge of when he's leaving. All I

know is he will be moved soon. The conversation

between the Sergeant and the officers comes to a whisper.

I turn to look around my cell; I recall it being about 6×8,

I'm standing in the middle of the cell, (standing) in-front of the door,

on the right is the concrete bed, this one was painted red,

on top was a blue pad folded in three located

on the corner nearest the door, to my immediate

left, concrete wall, the left back wall corner housed

the toilet/ water fountain/ wash station combo, a scratched

up Plexi mirror about four inches above it, the floor

was rough and so was the blue painted walls. I

walk over to the red concrete bed pulled the blue pad

and began unfolding it. It was a trifold pad just a smidgin

thicker than the sleeping mat I was issued

in the military. Finally, something to smile about.

The pad had a ton of cracks and rips,

reminding me of the plastic covered couches I

slept on growing up that would scratch

up my arms and legs making me hella ashy. I

sat on it and started feeling woozy right away.

I laid down. "Hey, no name, come here"

I rocked myself into a seated position

looked over at the cell door, it was one of the officers

from the computer desk. I put my slides on and walked

over to get a good look at the person holding me captive.

Upon approaching, I notice the officer is slender

with muscular arms, a short, bow-legged male,

who leans left. His head was a perfect ice cream cone

with ant like eyes a beak for a nose and very thin lips.

I smiled from the right side of my mouth

as I knew this gentleman

because I knew myself, I knew the offi-cer

in front of me awaiting my arrival

to the cell door. The door was painted

green with the setup of a sliding door, the top

and bottom sat on chains, in the middle of the door

is a slot in the shape of a rectangle big enough

for a personal pan pizza and it locked from the outside.

I remember arriving smooth as an ecstasy glide

(then) leaned into the corner of the door

and answered, "What did you ask?"

"Why don't you have a name listed, what is your name?"

"I'm nobody", is my reply to the officer's
question

"Why are you just a number? Where you
from?"

"I don't know C-", before I could finish,

A hurried voice from one of the cells

to the right of mines jumps

in, he's from the same place we are from.

"Aye, shut the muck up", is the officer's

reply to the voice, disappearing, only
ground

claps from his desert jungle boots,

give way his location. I go back

to the concrete bed and lay down before

leaving stage one of sleep, I overhear

the correction officer's debating

on who I am and my where I came from.

I smiled at the conversation and headed

for deeper sleep.

PART FOUR

The next morning came very fast

I heard the sound of the door slot

being opened, it was still dark

outside so I thought this must be dinner

or a late meal, one of the correction

officer's place a small carton and a Styrofoam

tray on the flap of the open-door slot.

"Get up and come this tray and juice",

was the CO words to me. I got up

and grabbed the Styrofoam and the carton of juice.

The officer slammed the slot like it was a door

of an old ass chevy blazer, before opening the tray,

I inspected the juice box; The box is red

with black lettering, packed with 150%

more vitamin C, Coupled with other vit-
amins

to help boost immune system. The name
escapes

my memory, but it was not juice but a
fruit punch

drink. I opened the drink for further
inspection,

it was clear as a Florida spring. The taste

still makes me smile, like freshly made
Kool-Aid

with cubes of ice (On the west this how
we start our day),

like fresh sweet tea with heavy ice on a
Southern day,

on the back where the ingredients are broken

down there was a disclaimer "Product

not for sale, still being tested". The front of the tray

was full of Corn Flakes, The two side pockets

held a cake the size of a little yellow sticky

note and the other a half of orange.

I quickly got up from the concrete bed

And rushed to the front if the cell " Aye big

dog, I need some milk", the guard

responded, "Okay bruh, I got you", I

went to my concrete bed and started

on my orange. I can hear the other inmates

yelling about milk. I turned and walked

to my aluminum water fountain slash toilet,

pushed the dime shape button then released

it, a tall thick stream of water shot out I

pushed the button a few more times, filled the Styrofoam

just up to the cereal (Every time I tell this story my heart feels explosive, my anger has me feeling nocturnal, I

feel like looking for these nugguhs and taking they muthafliggin

lives. This is how I feel, I thought I was different

somehow, anyway, keep reading.), the cereal separated revealing

the trays bottom. Being so caught up on milk I

didn't even think about something to eat with. The cereal

on the right (if looking from point of view) was soaking

up all the water so I stirred it with my fingers

until most of the cereal was mushy, I

guided the lower right corner of the tray to my mouth

and tilted it just before the mush got my mouth

the piece of cake hit my face right on the space

between my right eye and nose bridge slapping

on my right forearm and landing on my bottom part

of my coveralls, I quickly picked the cake up and smashed

it into my mouth, put the tray on the mat, ripped

a scooping piece out the top of the tray and spooned

that mushy ass cereal up and shook it down my throat,

it had a light metallic taste but filling. I overheard

the officer answering a time request from someone

in the same situation as me "430 in the morning". I

just remember going back to the sleep. Lunch

was done the same way, my tray con-
tained four slices

of white bread four thick slices of
bologna, In the two

corner slots of the tray was a cake (which
I mangled

first) in the other slot was shredded raw
cabbage pieces

and a red box fruit punch drink with a
150% vitamin C

"Officer I'm a vegetarian, can you get me
a different plate"

was out of my mouth before I thought
about it. "Oh, ok cool,

how long you been a vegetarian?" Replied the officer,

"A while now, it was hard to leave meat alone", I

said this with a perkier tone. "I am thinking about quitting

meat myself" the officer spoke while tugging up his pants.

I gave the officer a north and south then, the officer

points his left arm and says, "Lemme go to kitchen

and bring you back a veggie plate." "Coo, thank you",

after the dialogue, I returned to the concrete

bed and started making a sandwich out
of the white

bread and raw cabbage I left the four
thick slices

of bologna in the tray. Raw cabbage is
shitty

but the fruit punch drink with a 150%
vitamin C

helped my palette out. I was mimicking

the contestants of MLE (Major League
Eating)

The dinner tray came the same way, four
slices

of white bread with four thick slices of
bologna.

In the tray corner was two cookies the
other had shredded

raw cabbage. I looked up at the officer

as he was setting the red fruit punch
drink with 150%

vitamin C carton on flap of the open
slot, the officer made eye

contact and showed me all of his teeth,
the smile

from the officer ignited me, I know he
saw the fury

in my eyes because he slammed the slot
closed, "Get back

and eat your bologna" were his departing words.

PART FIVE

I have no idea how many days passed in my underground

cell as every day and meal, was the same. "Sir sir,

can you come speak to me for a minute" these words

came from a tall white man who copied his drip from Rick (the zombie killer with no flair).

I awakened from lunchtime slumber very groggy

seeing doubles, "Sir, please come to the door slot

and speak with me" the tall man repeated. I sat up

and took a minute to collect my thoughts, I turned looked

at the man with hair only on the sides of his head.

His shirt was white with blue vertical lines racing up to his collar,

the bottom of his shirt was tucked into his slim blue khakis.

I got up and walked to the open slot on the door and took a knee,

"Sir we have no information on you. Can we start

with your name, sir what is your name?" As the tall

man speaks, I am fascinated by how his head

could almost fit in the door slot. "Who are you?"

Was my reply while wiping my face down with my hands.

"I am a psychologist, and I was sent here to evaluate

you. Where are you from?" The psychologist spoke

this shaking his head and widening his eyes. "I'm

a staff sergeant in the US Army my unit is in Nevada, I

live in Las Vegas with my wife and kids. I was headed

back to Las Vegas when I was picked up by police. I

need to be released asap. I have respon- sibilities

that I have to tend to. Get me outta here." I

said this fast at least three times. The psychologist

rushed away as I was repeating my statement

for the fourth time saying, "Okay, okay, I

will contact the Army and let them
know we have you."

I was pacing in my cell until my dinner
tray

arrived. In my mind the sergeants who
brought me

here was full of shit. I decided it was
time for me

to go. I started planning what I was
going to do

when I was released and how I this was
going to go.

First, the sergeants would come get me and drive me

to another undisclosed location. There I

will be given another identity, some money,

and a vehicle. Tell me, "Stay away from Las Vegas

and anyone you may have known. We saved

you once, next time you are on your own",

I thought about driving off in a mirror-colored dodge viper.

While I was working out the details

of my release, breakfast trays where being distributed,

The officer walked pass my cell but didn't open my slot,

I wasn't worried about it because soon I

will be getting released with a new identity, cash,

and a car. After some time, I started banging

on the door calling for the officer. "What's up staff

sergeant," the officer says once he made it to the door.

"I'm supposed to be getting out today, any word?"

Was my reply. The officer smiles slow,

"You aint going nowhere, we checked

into the whole Army thing, they never heard

of you. You are a liar; we don't like liars."

I had no words for the officer, I was so confused,

my mind started twirling, I couldn't believe

they would deny me, what am I lying about? All

types of shit low-key started digging in my mind.

I said, "Fuck it", I got up off the concrete bed "I

need to eat, officer can I get my tray?"

This dude walked up to the cell door, "who are you?

Who sent you?" "What are you talking about,

look, look, my name is LUANIE LAM-BEY, I

am a staff sergeant in the United States Army. You

need to show some respect and get my tray." I

was in full drill sergeant mode when I spoke those words

to the officer. The officer stands up straight,

rolls his shoulders back, lines his arm down

an imaginary seam, and responded with, "Hoooah staff

sergeant, I will grab your tray and bring it back to you."

The officer returned with my tray in hand. He did not

open my slot though instead, the officer held it up

to the plexiglass with his left hand still standing

at attention and yells, " Your tray has arrived

staff sergeant," then he motions the tray towards me

and lets it go. The tray hit the ground hard

enough for the cornflakes to push its way out

of the tray. I lose it and tell that mother-fucker

to beat his fucking face, " Half RIGHT face, front lean

and rest position, move", the officer breaks his bearing

and get in a pushup position. My next command

went as follows; "I count the cadence you count

the repetition, begin.

A wun too tree",

The officer shouted, "One",

I continued, "A wun, too, tree"

The officer "Too",

Me, "A wun too tree",

The officer, "Three"

Me "Don't fuck with me"

The officer "Four"

Me "Don't, fuck, with, me"

The officer "Five"

Me "I will beat yo ass"

The officer "Six"

Me "Don't, fuck, with, me

The officer "Seven",

an officer about six foot dark but not black

with a sharp ass nose wearing a tactical

uniform comes 🏃 ☝. Drops into push up

position next to officer #1 and follows suit.

Me " I will punch your face"

Officers #1&2 "Eight"

Me "Don't, fuck, with, me"

Officers #1&2 "Nine"

Me "A WUN, TOO, TREE"

Officers #1&2 "TEN"

Me (melodic) "Recover" then I said "Relax".

The officers pop to attention and responded

to the command simultaneously "NEVER".

The rest of the day is fuzzy but I do remember

the Dr Morty coming by an telling me they still

have no idea who I am. I received no meals

throughout the day just different offi-cer's

asking me about my life, duty stations,

and how come I don't exist. I do not recall

if the sun was still rising or on its way to setting. I

recall yelling at the four officers and Dr Morty

outside my cell door. I called one of the female officers

a bitch and promised retribution if I
wasn't fed

and released. The quad of officers left
and upon

returning happened to be fully dressed
in riot gear;

Face, body, and arms shields. So, I got
ready, too nugguh,

I flooded the cell with water from my
aluminum toilet, I

splashed shit everywhere: The floor the
walls my fucking

concrete bed. Afterwards, I stuffed it
with a roll of shit paper

I've yet to use and flushed tell that bitch look like a lagoon. I

took my coveralls off, wrapped each leg part

around my wrist, grabbed my bed pad and got real fucking

small and waited. Inhale, exhale, inhale, exhale, inhale, exhale,

inhal- I hear a pop then, zzzzzzz the fuckers...

(Side bar/ I recall a black officer tall brother at a minimum six two, bald head favor Keenan in *Lowdown Dirty Shame*. We made eye contact I said, "bruh please bruh help me bruh please bruh I haven't eaten, my people my people don't even know I'm here, bruh please bruh, you wrong bruh you wrong my brotha you wrong" that nugguh just took a deep breath and lowered his head.)

Shot a taser through the slot. Each shot

sounded like somebody was breaking a light bulb

one by one. After about three tries of trying to tase

me through my bed mat. I heard some-thing different

hit me bed pad. It sounded like water directly

from the hose or when going through the car wash

while the car is in neutral, the sound it makes when the rinse

water is hitting the windshield. I was confused, then my eyes

and the area around it started feeling like I irritated it

with sea sand at the north end of Daytona beach

during the weekend of my birthday

which I celebrate in the middle

month of a southern summer. I took slow deep

breaths until I could no longer stop my chest

from opening up. My face from my nose

down was covered with mucus and baa-
baa, all of it thin

and thick. I buried my faced inside my
wet coveralls

making sure to wet down my eyes and
inhaled deep

until my chest could no longer rise.
"Eeehhhhaa" the door

to my cell jerks open. I'm thinking this is
my fucking

chance, my fucking chance to get the
fuck out of here,

and go home, and fuck EVERYBODY
up. I heard

the swoosh of the water which gave away their positionings,

like the two bandits in *Home Alone (2)*, I listened

and took deep dark breaths and focus on my cue to move. I

ejected across my concrete bed by placing my right foot

against the cum infested, booger infested, dried sputum

cold wall, with the pad providing front cover. When my middle

front toes touched a little corner of the edge. Using the pad

to help me gage the location of my
obstacles. I leap sideways

with the pad leading the way. I lay out on
two of the four

intruders, they stumbled into the wall. I
popped up

on my feet and started swinging fierce, I
maxed out

the first crack-a I seen coming in the
door third

behind the two weh catch it first.
(check), He catch

a front kick, I lifted my right knee mid-
line of my shoulders

and POW, one good fuck lick. I thrusted my lower

back forward to complete the motion then pop my leg

back. I turned right and proceeded to fatigue the mid-section

of the second buster to enter the room "I jabs up the mon",

with ferocious body shots "Yah am, yah am, yah am" finished him

with my signature knee to the face. Turned to the right

for the lead man. I see him retract his shield. I

heard the sound of to light bulbs being broken

simultaneously. I start dancing off top, I remember

wishing my God had given me wings (on some Gargoyle ish).

Ooohh ohh oohh. Ahhhj ahhhh aahhhhh aaahhhahhhh"

They moved in and started whaling on me, I was trying to swing

but the current flowing from the tasers had all my attention. I

started low crawling like Dave Chappelle in the Rick James skit through waves of feet and fist. I finally crawled out the scuffle,

when my right lower arm felt crushed, it was a black tactical

boot. I grabbed the boot with my left arm. I felt the tip

and followed the steel right past the toes. The pressure

from the officer standing on my arm prompt me to act fast. I

bit down on the boot like a snake, hoping to break skin. The officer

screamed like a bitch, "He's biting my foot"

then, takes a knee and starts to ground and pound my head

into the concrete floor. I let go after the fifth hammer

fist, looked up towards the door, there standing in the doorway

with a camera aimed at me was Dr. Morty. I was relieved

to see him, before I passed out, I yelled " Thank God

you got this on camera", everything went black.

PART SIX

I opened my eyes, seeing the Dr. And officers circled

around me, at the same time I see my hands tied

on each side and my feet were tied together. I

was on some kind of wooden bed/gur-ney,

only thing was free was my head. The Sgt I

called a bitch earlier, looked at me and gave one

of the officers a command, "Go get the spit bag

and put it on him". I didn't know what the spit

bag looked like, but I knew it wasn't good

by the look that accompanied the command. "No,

no, please, listen I'm telling the truth. I live in Las Vegas,

I have four kids, I have a wife, please, you don't

have to do this." I felt my voice raising to a loud plea,

"I just came back from Afghanistan, I

have had over 450 successful missions how dare

you'll do this, I have fought for my country three times

why, why, why, I am a veteran I fought for you," tears

and snot makes the whole scene blurry. All of a sudden,

I could see only straw stitching and the light

shining in showing squiggly silhouettes. "Ahhh ahhhh ahhh

no, please release me, don't do this you don't have to do

this, what you are doing is wron-", the pressure on my neck,

cuts my vocals short. I feel the inch and a half shoelace string becoming a part of the skin on my neck. The officer was determined

to merge the lace and my neck. I felt like someone was holding

me under water. My mouth moistened, my eyes refused to close,

my core had contracted causing me to sit up while, the officer

was behind me on a knee, pulling the bag that was over

my head down by the strings. " God please protect my family"

was my last thought before death. I gave up my ghost

and all hope, everything became dark. I

came to, still wearing the bag this time I was strapped

into a chair. "Aahhh ahhhh let me out, let me out

ahhhhh ahhhh, let me go, stop this, let me go", the words

came soft from my water mouth diluted with hemoglobin,

the pool of fluid building inside my mask felt mad sticky

like Now&Later spit. It goes dark in my spit bag again. I woke

up to a view of my arm pits, my feet off the ground, my ankles are loose, my big toes and the ones next to it still have a relationship

with the ground. My wrists are cuffed together and clipped

into a D-ring. I see the two sergeants that drove me

here from the freeway. This was a different part the jail

I was in. This room reminded me of an Iraqi interrogation

room. The officer's spoke to me as if they were a duet,

going back and forth between them, occasionally,

turning to face me and ask questions. The words

that were spoken have yet to gain volume in memory. I

know whatever they asked me was important. I know I

didn't respond to their questions; I was in shock. I

thought my country was on my side, they cannot

be if I'm hanging from the ceiling in handcuffs while the two mudsuckers

I successfully completed missions with, question me. My

mannerisms were like the King of England's when the princess

revealed she was prego for William Wallace. My mouth

wouldn't open. The two officers started to fatigue my body.

My ribs stood in place of the freezer meat destroyed in *Rocky* (1).

From this beating came my most hurtful statement, "Okay,

okay, I will tell anything you want to know". My words

came out like I was asking for an inhaler. One of my assailants smirked and held up a fist. This halted the other assailant

who had a forearm placed midclavicular to my chest. I'd imagine,

to keep me steady for a powerful swing. The officer mouthed,

"Say wah" smiled and stepped in closer as if receiving

an award, from the base commander. "I will tell you whatever

you want to know", is what came out of my windpipe. I

am not sure if I gave up whatever it was, they

were asking for, but I must have, they stopped beating

my ass. I sung like Whitney did with her sister

in that cabin scene in the *Bodyguard*.

PART SEVEN

These next couple of chapters are the most blurred

and traumatizing memories to relive. My

next memories came back in my cell

on my concrete bed. I wasn't awake

much after the debriefing, just spurts

of moments when the guards would wake

me and punish me for not eating any of the trays.

They tek me BOTTY a few times, it was that little

muthafucka, the officer who "Dropped" my cereal,

while his partner used my face as a sparring glove. I

would be woken up by this enormous pressure

destroying my backside, not being able to gather strength

to fight physically but, battle spiritually with my soul. My

head would be off the concrete bed hanging, I

remember looking at the officer laying into my face

with his fist, I looked him right in his sark eyes,

the bottom of my neck would be hyper extended

like I was praying to my god and all I remember,

the punches hitting my orbits on both sides of my face.

At some point, I would just pass the fuck out. Nights I

don't remember being fucked in my ass, they

would come in and drag me by legs until my body

hit the concrete floor. Oh yeah, since my return

to my cell, up to this point, I had no blanket or bed pad.

Throw uneaten trays on me, I remember

being covered in smelly ass bologna and dry

ass cereal, then one would pick me up

and they would recreate a scene from *House*

Party when Kid got socked out in the lunchroom. I

don't know why they stopped but they stopped

coming in my cell at night. One night, I heard deep

screams like my man from the movie with the girl

from the *Poker Face* song. My senses told me

it was close. I was laying on my concrete bed

in the last position my abuser left me, prostrating

towards them, arm off to the side, one of them hanging

off the side of the concrete bed. I recall all around my

booty hole burning so bad. I put my fingers in my mouth

and tried to moisten it with spit then I reached back

and winch at the touch of my tiger maimed ass hole. I

repeated this a couple of times until all the scabs

around my anus were moistened. I was relieved

that night.

PART EIGHT

My next memories in that cell are about healing

myself while still in and out of consciousness. I

was in a wheelchair being pushed somewhere I

had my eyes open but all I saw was black. I

felt for my eyes and was met by stiff swollen

meat, my eyes had a thick leather scab

along the lining of my eye lids. "I'm sorry

men, it shouldn't have went down like
that" was softly

spoken into me ear by the person pushing my

wheelchair. The image that popped into
my

head was that the black officer who I
told he wrong,

had been pushing my wheelchair (I don't
know for sure

if it was him but, I like to think it was
him). I said nothing

just listened for where I might be headed. We ended up

in a room, I correctly assumed was the courtroom,

because a voice that reminded my ears of the chicken

with seven spices and herbs was saying something

to someone about understanding the plea agreement

the person was entering and was he under any controlled

substances or mentally competent. I wondered if my

family was in the courtroom and was I getting out today. I

felt some hope rising in my stomach, I smiled and said

internally, "I am going to get some pussy tonight". Then I

get rolled back to a cell. A familiar childhood voice says,

"Open your eyes staff sergeant, I need you to see me". I

sat up and popped my eyes lids open without acknowledgement

of the pain. I felt nothing but extreme alertness

as if nothing happened to me. It was a guy

that was identical to my man who put his thing

in an apple pie. I looked up at him, " Sergeant, I am one

of your lawyer's. I'm sorry about this misunderstanding,

we will take care of this for you. In the meantime,

get yourself ready to get back in the fight", this was expressed

with such clarity. I had no words for the lawyer not even

when he asked if I had any questions. Looking back, I

was thinking that I would be good because they now know

who I am. If the white guy in a fitted blue suit and red tie

say he is going to take care of everything, I'm the nugguh

that is going believe him. I don't remember the proceedings

in court, just that my lawyer said I was pleading not guilty.

JUNE

These mutha-fuckers always win, omg, how could I not break.

THE ROAD 2 RECOVERY

Three times a charm!

Didn't die overseas but mentally I was gone

still I was able to remain smooth like balm.

I was raging on the inside

no one can ever know, I must remain calm.

Dreams and civilian actions fertilized my lawn

thoughts of death grew stronger like twenty-three

in the paint, it couldn't be stopped,

mental LeBron.

Abandoned my family and so-called

friends too, No one understood anyway,

I wanted my life to be through.

Reached out for help but then again not
really,

didn't want to seem less than,

a staff sergeant has to be BETTER,

INDESTRUCTIBLE,

to let them in would be worst then suicide.

Finally, I got lucky instead of death I

got blessed with jail,

too bad I wouldn't see it,

To me, it just slowed down the clock

to an early death, released

and guess what, now, I'm homeless!

Under the bridge nex to the arena, is my bedroom,

it's huge, I allowed others to sleep here too,

downtown at *Lake Eola* became my living room,

I allowed others to hang out here too,

no money, no food, no mind, I felt like I had no time.

Two in the morning next to a payphone off

Church and Terry. No one to call, not anyone

who would answer anyways, wait, on the side

there   is   a   sticker   it   read
1-800-273-8255,

I reached for the phone, dialed the number,

someone answered, I took a deep breath,

"Hello, I need help". Thank God

for the red, white and blue, pick up the
phone

and dial Veterans please let your country help you,

the ones that help, have had similar experiences,

they know what to do, God

bless America, Please God, bless our Veterans,

we need you,

Peace.

https://youtu.be/Zx2TLgdC1-E

SAD

The heavy silence

erases good deeds

with its length,

resentment seeps

through my skins

pores like air through

a vent,

it has a filthy

scent, can't

be heaven

sent, it can't

be a blessing

lent.

FEBRUARY

This week was crazy busy, guess what? I am no longer homeless, yes! It is taking a while to truly sink in, that's okay, it will, I have been homeless (for) four years, I have not lived alone, even longer, I'm anxious, I'm doing a great job at being cool, well, just being humble about it, I want to say fuck you, look what I got, cuss some people out, I have decided to let my actions do the talking for me, so far so good, things at work are calm, I'm no longer the new guy, I gave Maccara my number and email we talked for a little, then she said her phone broke, even though she's always on it, lol, crazy right but, it'd works for her, we lie for no reason sometimes, I told two lies last week, okay three, it's okay, this week, I'm shooting for zero, didn't speak to NUNU (my oldest daughter) this week, phone troubles, I'm speaking to Xhena again it's getting easier to let her go, I'm over her, she's planning on a summer visit every day, I feel different about finally having sex with her, there's something telling me to be careful dealing with her in that way, that dream of me turning her down, to me, is a sign, if she does come and sex happens, condom is a must, I hope I am strong enough to reach for it, I will be, I know it, I'm strong enough now, I had dinner with Cia, I really like her, she likes me a lot, when I look at her soul I see truth, no lies that I can see, dinner was amazing we shared food and spoke for a little over an hour about everything, it flowed so natural we even shared our poems, it was beautiful, baby girl has skills, she was so nervous, I love this girl('s) fearlessness, reminds me of a young Xhena, I wonder if she senses how much I like her, King (my oldest son) and I had (a) great conversation, I should be spending time with him in March this reunion will be very emotional the last time seen him he was fake sleep, he looked so big, older by many years, I wonder if he (is) in on it (the plot to get me to sacrifice myself for the world). Didn't think I would see him again til after he turned eighteen, everything is happening so fast, I love it. Thanks for listening.

DEEP

I'm angry this morning,

I'm an open cup,

waiting on the enemy

to pour in some wine,

"Desert for me please".

RAN-DOUGH

The playoffs are here,

I usually, rep a different

team every year,

my skin is brown

as a bear,

DEATH has given me

a thousand-yard stare.

APRIL

Did my first poetry show in 3 years maybe longer, it felt like the first time I ever stepped on that stage, it took a lot out of me, drain(ing), not in a tired way, just the focus it takes is mind blowing, I have really been paying attention to me, something is happening, I'm hearing people's thoughts a lot louder, still, working on not fighting it, takes a lot of energy to suppress, I'm watching everyone real carefully wondering what side are they on, I wonder is Cia an enemy, is that the reason this beautiful woman keeps so close. I

have so much power, yet I refuse to acknowledge who is who (for) real, I keep her close because, I know who sees what she wants from me, what they all want from me, no, not even close, I explored myself this week didn't feel like I thought it would, didn't feel like anything actually, this chapter is very interesting. Tanks for listening.

BAD DAYS

Bad days, are far and few, between,

On this daily, grind of, chasing C.R.E.A.M,

The nightmares, the nightmares, are the only consistent

thing.

Death is what's mostly playing in my dreams,

in that land, this rhyme has no scheme,

observe my eyes, it has no gleam,

I am chunky, pants popping at the seams,

Nose blowing out heavy steam,

tears coming at a steady stream,

with my hands I cover my face then I scream,

the baddie next to me wraps her arms around me and says meekly, "Baby it was just a dream".

Though, her face looks like the *Painful Smile meme,*

mind in slow motion, like it off that lean,

still, this nigga smiles, cuz, I stack that Green.

Bad days, are far and few, between,

on this daily, grind of, chasing C.R.E.A.M,

the nightmares, the nightmares, -R-

a consistent thing.

SKA LyingTongue Vol.3

F.E.A.R

Fear has me thinking

clear,

with the instints

of a deer.

Fear has me putting away

my old eyes and

screwin' in a new pair, sprayed

with *Rain-X*, even in humid

weather, they still clear. False Evidence
Apearing

Real that's f.e.a.r.

UNDERNEATH

I cant take another

secret, PLEASE,

if you know

something

about

ME,

speak IT, dont keep IT.

JULY

Nothing is going as expected but just (th)e way I want it, nothing (I) have chosen have eluded me, I have decided that Cia is not a player in this game, we are not a like, as she watches and studies my every move, I often catch them still watching, doesn't bother me as much, I am

super accepting, as I write this I realized that I always loved the camera, some of my best moments was when I (k)new they were rolling, now that I know eyes are watching at all times, I am starting to get use to it, the fact, I am an actor a star, when it is time to die on the screen I shall, Thanks for listening.

ME

I am afraid, so scared I cry, death

is near death is here, I know you, all

of you, I have seen you before,

interacted with you before. You

have nothing new for me to explore,

how dare you say you love me

and still play this game of pretend,

you are not who you say you are, I

don't know your true name so, I

call you enemy, you stay close to me,

unable to kill me, I am your captive, you

prefer the word guest, I will not die for
you,

any of you, I am so done playing your

game, this whole thing is fake, my

girl, my life, children, my success,

this is all one big show, who is watching?

I am the way, the light, you feel you

should follow me, fear has you, fear has
me

See fear had me white out my own piece,
PEACE.

MARCH

I am a week overdue, I know, I am running from something and calling it
not having a enough time to write,
now that I am done telling myself
that lie, I would like to speak on

something, when I started this journal it was to speak on the things that are deep down inside me that, I felt that I could not speak to anyone else about. I have not done that, just on superficial things, this doesn't sit well with me, I am hiding even though, they are trying hard not to be here, they are watching, reading, observing everything, I am ignoring them, doing a great job at it, they are not doing a great job hiding or is it because, I know they're there in plain site, I feel them, I wonder when they will reach out to me again, what instruction will they give, maybe that's what makes me special, the fact that I have no instructions, I literally do and say what I want, wow, is that why many hate me, because of this, do they feel

I am not taking full advantage, that I am not worthy of such a privilege, do I feel I am not worthy, is that why I don't take advantage, I was told not to abuse this but, how can I know what abuse really is, if I don't push it. Thanks for listening.

HOPE FOR PEACE

I hope no one is listening

when, I know

for a fact

they heard me,

I hope no one sees me

when, I know

everything in my

body feels their eyes,

I hope no one gossips to me

when, my heart shutters

at their remarks.

I hope to speak no

evil,

I hope to see no

evil

I hope to hear no

evil,

I hope the devil

receives my resistance

poem.

PROJECTION

It's brady how pain

can be push

through the phone,

shot gun to da dome,

leave you feelin'

lumpy as a scone,

homeless but livin'

in a home.

CLUB KNIGHTS

At the club standing at the bar

waiting to order a drink,

when he is approached

by a person,

Person: Mem-bah mee?

Person ordering the drink: No bwoi, yuh have da wrong mon.

Person ordering the drink turns around and point's

at the bartender. Three shots ring out

and the person ordering a drink,

forehead projected brains resembling

an anus with explosive diarrhea. The person

ordering the drink hits the bar chin

first then, he gives into the ground.

The end

FINESSE

Where the cash

at, where that bag

at, I got my bags

packed, I'm

willing to fly

for that, stealth

drones fly

for that, I've

had soldiers,

that died

for that, I've

lost my mind

for that, where the cash

at, where that bag

at, American's

need that, I'm

caught in a money

TRAP.

ABOUT THE AUTHOR

Luanie   Lion   BlessUp   Lambey-
Bermudez

I am a father of six children (maybe 7, I have a loose Cock), a husband to a loving, intelligent, beautiful wife. I am a poet at heart who uses different mediums to express that poetry. Twelve years of military service has left me with scars that can and cannot be seen. After a severe mental break, homelessness, and years of being in the care of the VA, I was finally able to get back on my feet. I now live on the Left Coast in Sizzle Town. I am a creator of conversation and promoter of personal growth. Over 10 years as an established poet, writer, serial-expressionist, and magazine editor. I completed bachelor's degree at University of Central Florida and currently enrolled in a master's program at University of Nevada, Las Vegas. BlessUp

CHAPTER 2

BIPOLAR

LUANIE LION BLESSUP LAMBEY-BERMUDEZ

INNER SPEAK

Struggles of self-destruction

is tattooed on different

sections of my skin,

Struggles of failure

is the natural cologne

seeping through my pores,

Struggles of love

is scars outside of my iris,

enticing anyone

that looks within.

JUNE

I let the stresses and the pressures of this world get to me, I really did, lol, I wanted to so, I let it. I allowed myself to feel it so much, my body reacted to the stress very well, I came up with a cold sore in my nostril, kind of alarming, I prayed with Cia, it was an eye opener for her, she plays her part well, they all do, even me, thanks for listening.

DEAR BLACK PEOPLE

I am speaking to you today not as a white person, but as a brother.

Not the type of brother that has shared the same mother,

but as a brother of tragedy and as a shared member of trauma.

Although, the trauma black people have faced

is significant.

I assure you the trauma white people have faced are different, but on equal playing fields.

Dear black people,

your race has endured a generational state of oppression.

First through chains, followed by the mind, and eventually the spirit.

Traumatic stress runs in your bloodstream.

The pillaging, beatings, raping's, false incrimination, and murdering's of your ancestors

still linger in your DNA.

My father is a housing developer, his father was a school teacher, his father was a police officer, his father was a correction officer, his father was a bounty hunter, and his father was an overseer on a plantation.

I sat down with my late great grandfather and he told stories, not the ones told at Christmas or family gatherings about heroism and triumph.

He conversed about the things that had been done to keep us superior in a country that was slowly becoming un pure.

I was told stories of shootings, hangings, beatings, burnings, raping's, and cleansings that he said were terrifying but, necessary.

That day, I realized the agenda of my family, — we were at war with the other race. I also learned that I had traumatic stress flowing in my blood stream.

Dear black people,

a soldier goes to war for the country.

The soldier is told: this is for your loved ones overall, the survival of the nation.

The soldier embraces a mindset that the enemy is inhuman. If the soldier was to take a moment to stop and think that this is another human being, the soldier would no longer be able to continue.

In privacy, that soldier reflects on the past. Dreams reveal that the actions were against human beings.

This is the pre-cursor of traumatic stress disorder. With that, I started to understand that oppression whether, the oppressed or the oppressor affected both sides in a harmful way.

I was informed, that even though they

laughed like us, had the same organs as us, bleed the same colors as us as confusing as this may sound, during this war of keeping America great and progressing we were the humans and they were not.

Dear black people,

I spent the majority of my time on this earth looking away, issues that seemed racially charged I just simply turned my head.

I drove to hip hop (new and old), partied to trap music, and sometimes ended the night with company, vibing to Rhythm and Blues.

I associate with plenty of black people

and would even consider some as friends.

At parties when a song says the n word, I would say it too and look at them not in an intimidating manner, more permissive. (they would smile)

I am on a path to healing myself, hoping my peers follow.

James Baldwin said, "if white people learned to love themselves and each other, then the Negro problem would no longer exist."

Dear black people, we are working towards understanding you and that is the first step towards loving you.

PKA LyingTongue

APRIL

Wtf am I doing? I don't know, I am crying because I am hurting, or I just admitted to myself that I have a problem, I love pain, issues guide me, my plans have shifted, I know it is for the better or it would not be, it is so hard, I am allowing myself to be what I must, I am allowing myself to change into something I do not wish to be, I do not want to give a fuck about others or anything, I do not want to love anything other than me, I hate these people in my world, The reality is to hate is to care to care is to love, I am going to set new goals with my partner, new goals with myself, new goals with my

children, The change is met with resistance internally, my mouth is talking smoothly as it often does, Thanks for listening peace.

WRUN KNIGGAW

Wrun, Kniggaw run; Babylon ah ketch U yah fuk;

Wrun, kniggaw run; Dah airport dis way.

Wrun, Kniggaw run; Babylon ah ketch U Yah fuk;

Wrun, Kniggaw run, N-2-Gawd, U ah get way.

Dis Kniggaw run like da son of a gun,

Da street full of cars so he snatch him
wun;

He knock 2 cars, hop out, and start
wrun;

He wrun fast, but Babylon "kill fa fun".

Dat Kniggaw can wrun,

Dat Kniggaw can fly,

Babylon lick 2shots af tah da mon,

They missed both times, eh say,

"Bets, Dat Kniggaw can wrun. He out
wrun me gun".

MAY

They played it perfect, crying as if for me, I cried as I notice the emotional hold those people have on me that I allow (them) to have on me, speaking about it now has my head aching, I feel a new poem, I love my children so much, even if its not real, to go through this this game is the ultimate tear jerker, to know that the game is that deep that people can act so well, is amazing, I played my part well, outstanding, I just let my emotions play, it was not as hard, yes it was, last night Cia made a statement that roused me up so bad I just wanted to scream "fuck you and this game all of you", I held it in, instead, I said something else, I feel like they are trying me all the

time from far back, what I am working on understanding is how come,
what is the reason for me to be
angered, what are they looking for,
Its defeating to think about the truth
that I have come across, I am not
done having fun, getting exactly
what I ask for, that part does something for me, I love it thanks for listening.

SUICIDE

Stomach contracts

at the thought of life,

Tears flow steady

at the thought of life,

Phony laughs never

become real,

open wounds never

heal, ANGER is how I

feel, Insecure about how I

feel or even what's real.

JUNE

I am starting (to) run faster now, this world reality is starting (t)o become more prevalent, I am still catching their eyes on me, the audience likes Cia and I relationship, she has not left yet, still part of the story, thanks for listening.

BIPOLAR

I have a pulsing strain

on the left side of my neck,

I bring people in never

for the best,

The strain starts halfway

above my right

STRESS.

FEBRUARY

I have so much to tell you, I am ecstatic, elated, hanging out with Cia has been magical, she is truly one of a kind and special, I love her, I know she loves me, even past the game I sense it, she told me who she really is, that feel special, it's deep, she a great actor, she makes me feel like it's all real, like she's real, when I am with her, I forget that I am a player in this vicious game, I am loving it though, it's becoming very enjoyable and of course, since Cia and I have been intertwined, the women must smell the semen, they flock, Cia will be leaving Friday, it's bittersweet, I (have) chosen to put somethings on the back burner until she leaves, I am going to miss her, I think I finally found someone who knows what to do with me, I also had a moment of growth when Xhena called to tell me about a conversation she had with Danice, I told her I was not going to give it any energy but, after I got off the phone with her, I did give some energy, I was upset and hurt, it took some time eventually, I worked through it, I realized that they are still my biggest haters and that I need people like them to let me know I am progressing to the next level, it's amazing, I'm really growing, my potential knows no boundaries, I seen *Split* (a movie) and it reinforced what I already knew, that, I can get to the sun, When I spoke to Smush (my youngest boy), he asked for clothes and shoes which, had his mom written all over it. I feel like she wants him to feel disappointed with me, like he is not giving her enough credit, I just kept it real with him, the truth always find a way to make it alright, Work has been awesome I

like it there. Thank you for listening.

FREEDOM

"The power or right to act, speak, or think as one wants without hindrance or restraint" – Merriam Webster

"Doing, saying, being what you choose without regards for how others feel and/or think about it" – LIONBLESSUP

That gun was in my face,

I looked down the barrel

It was as dark as the soul that possessed it.

ME:

"What did I do sir?"

"Please, what did I do?"

BABYLON:

"Shut the fuck up!

I will tell you, what you didn't do.

That man, that needed a ride that day when it was raining.   You gave him one.

That woman, that would have never known how it felt to be loved. You gave it to her.

That man, that felt insecure about his manhood. You showed him yours.

That lady, that felt like the gas station is the best she can do. After that hundred you put in her hand for her customer service, she knew.

That man, who wanted his own shop. You made him look you in your eyes and speak it into existence.

when he told you, he deserved it.   We heard it.

The hugs you constantly give to men who not worth it,

The loving you continuously give to women who have not earned it,

The money you loosely hand out to people who did not work for it,

WE observed it.

Listen to me, NIGGA,

You can't go around smiling,

facing all your fears,

sharing knowledge with all your peers,

head held high

giving off much cheer,

seeming as if you see the world so clear,

like you successful,   You have not sold a
single poem this year,

This is AMERICA,

You are an AMERICAN.

Meaning:

You are not allowed to act like that,

You are not allowed to be like that,

You are not allowed to do things like that,

The only thing you are entitled to in this country,   is

freedom. So, stay within yours.

PKA LyingTongue

HAPPY VETERANS DAY

To all my Vets including their Spouses.

HAPPY Veterans Day to my past,

to my bloodline in World War II,

Great gran we here thanks

to your husband, Mr. Diego, I

salute you, your crew kept one side of
Korea,

off the other side of Korea's doorstep.

To my peoples that served in Vietnam

that look like me, I

heard you dropped bombs on all yo
opps

not just the VC, my uncle Post would
read his Bible

before cutting on music and watching
TV,

take a pause, chug his gin, and share war
stories

with me, then he would turn up the
music

loud and take a next drink.

To REPTILE and his band of brothers

for training the TEUFEL HUNDEN

down in Belize, you helped the US
Marines

put the gorilla's warfare at ease,

why we was in Panama that's yet to be
seen,

even in another

country my family bled army green,

Garifuna warriors are a rough, and
tough,

fighting machine. That's on the HUNTA
mon,

we slayed.

(Happy Veterans Day)

To all my shipmates that was in the bay

that day (9/11), still don't understand
how the planes

got taken over that way, member how
the officer

ran into the bay, screaming, "we going
to war

today, we going to war I say, get your shit

together shipmates, now's not the time

to delay, we going to war today, all

terrorist have to pay".

(Happy Veterans Day)

To all my hospital recruits, in 2001

I was you, after six months of training

A great responsibility was put on me too, I

was there too, big up to my people in Chicago

who push Thanksgiving dinner back a day or two, you

waited for me to be able to join you, this Veteran

will never forget you.

(Happy Veterans Day)

To all my hospital Apprentices, aint no fun being

at fleet marine school, learning how to operate

as marines do, extra military instruction for clowning

with my crew, I spent the day with a Montford Point

marine, one of the last survivors of the first

all-black crew, they was led by a serious du,

Hashmark Johnson had more stripes then movies

featuring Richard Bronson, camp Johnson

special blessings to you. (S.I.P HM MYO)

(Happy Veterans Day)

To all the hospital man in pharm tech

school, College in the service was so cool,

never in a million years did I think I

had the smarts to make it through, a
hundred

drugs a week, plus the indications, con-
traindications,

adverse reactions, and side effects too,
not to mention

dosing for infants, yeah, we had to cal-
culate

that too, but I did that, graduated number eleven

solid with a ninety-two, shout to my
cousin's

in VA, I miss you dudes.

(Happy Veterans Day)

To Naval hospital in Charleston

On rivers Avenue, with you is where I

learned what real brotherhood could
do,

the love brothers showed me, proved
southern

hospitality is truth, the claps you gave
my first poetry

show stuck like glue, downtown next to
Bubba Gumps

Shrimp was where they sold and hung
SLAVES,

to all the spirits yelling in my ear, my
hearing

was cut off but just know I felt you.

(Happy Veterans Day)

To all the divisions of Marines

The unit I was in is now Fourth MLG

Back in the day it was FSSG,

That time was tough, I didn't know
what to pack

for war, thinking back I took a lot of
stuff:

two seabags a ninety-pound ruck a
medical bag

that clocked in at 40lbs, and a backpack
full of abstract stuff,

In Germany, the CO said, "If you can
buy it,

you can drink it, we are going to defend

our country, no one's gonna have fuss.",

Kuwait was hot, inside of the tent was
hotter,

think the release would come from
drinking

water, don't bother, "Dah wah-tah hot.",

the only way to cool it down was in a
black

sock, outside of combat I filled my head
with Too $hort,

stuffed my belly with meals ready to eat, fed

my spirit by singing with the choir, we built

a makeshift stage, the boards was hella loose. I

filled my lungs with a Blizzle, the people with dibs

in it, numbered about six. Thank Every-one's

God, we made it back.

(Happy Veterans Day)

To all my dawgs I was with in Iraqi,

that first night, was a mass cass,

I didn't think we'd make it out,

somehow, we stayed strong

like a stout, "Once you hear the whistle

it's too late, Jus say yuh pray-ahs

and hope that the good Lawd

cut you a break.", "Catch em' if you can.",

is a favored phrase, incoming is consistent so, aint no sleep

takin' place, Rip-Its, poetry and my
brother's steadied

me in the, make it home race, I can
never forget

how war taste; metallic and dirty, I

could call it gamey. The way back home
was sweet

and wack, imagine going home and
your ride gettin'

shot at, the gunner called it fast "SAF 3
O'CLOCK",

the pilot leaned the nook right then the
gunner

let the fifty take flight, "Target do- RPG"
the windows

and the opening in the back, allowed me
to see the close

impact, thank heavens the gun ship circle back,

before we left the area, I saw the building collapse, shout

out to my flyboys', they handled that.
The good Lawd

was with we, so, we made it back.

(Happy Veterans Day)

To all my battles posted in the KBC

if you lost that's Afghanistan G,

the drama when we came in was like the
beginning

of COD, shout out to all gunners, mines
was my eyes

at night, we displayed a hard target all
night, never dropped

down during a fight, my crew was hype,
a robot,

my MAT-V, about six M.R.A.P's, and a
plethora of whites,

is how we traveled most nights, member
our last trip to BAF

(Bagram Air Field) that night ended bad.
None of my soldiers died

so, I'm glad, but, other soldiers died and
for that I'm sad,

that night I boo boo'd in my fart sack
bad, those rockets

literally scared the shit out my ass, slid
off to the latrines

smooth and slow, showered off all the
doo, I still smelt

like fecal though, who cares we made it
back.

(Happy Veterans Day)

To all the veterans who thought about
suicide

today but, didn't act,

My life is like an empty revolver with
one round in it, every day

I get up I grab the chamber and spin it,
the days I

shoot myself I can't see myself winning,
those be the days I

know the devil is grinning, those be the
days I

feel like sinning,

grabbing my opp by the neck and start
pinging

their face with the point of my fist

But, I don't, Instead, I go smoke, get on
the phone

and call HOPE, turn on Martin and
laugh at a Pam

joke, take my meds and ten minutes
later I turned coat, I'm

relaxed, no longer want smoke, brought
all my personalities

together and took a vote, we now are
one I

feel a lot better, eighteen months of
counseling gave me tools

for bad weather. Shout out to the support

provided by the VA. My government
came through for me,

in a major way.

(Happy Veterans Day)

Spouses, Children, Shipmates (USN),
Hard dogs (USMC),

Airmen (AF), and Battle buddies (US
Army)

I Lion BlessUp, salutes you.

ANSWER

Why did I join the military, because I

was a Pussy.

APRIL

I got my nips pierced it hurts real bad, I don't know, let me stop, I am so much more appealing to my eyes the human eyes, I spoke with my family, they all say they missed me and I said I missed them, I lied, I don't miss them, not one, I really do not miss my kids that much, it crazy in my mind, kind of sound wrong, insane, if anyone was to ever find out this fact, o'well, lately, I have not been diving to deep, things have been shallow, I am allowing this superficial life to guide me, not really, I am facing fears still little by little, I am on track to greatness, afraid to really levitate, so, I engulf my time in working (on) poetry and working out, I am a poet, yet, I feel like much more, how much longer, thanks for listening, I know they are waiting for me to blow the whistle, I am having so much fun getting what I want.

RAMBLING

I swear I don't want control,

I swear I want all control,

make a choice? Who says I have to make one,

I'm free,

I have the ability to say I want something

one minute and say I don't the next,

Truth be told my truth is always told, even if it sounds

different from yours, I feel the change oozing

out my pores, I call it a slow leak redemption,

I have learn that to yourself is the only person

to who you need repent. I have forgiven myself

and still continue to do so, my past shows me

that in the end I'm all I got. People live

to disappoint, put your hopes in any-thing

other then you and the lesson will be yours

to learn, I'm here, there, I'm everywhere

so, I'm nowhere, call me God, what if I

was to tell you that you are your own prophet

would you believe me, if I told you that you had the power

to predict your own future, would you believe me,

if I told that you are a special being, not only can you

predict, you can create, didn't dude say ye are all Gods,

WE are all everywhere at onetime yet nowhere

at one time, what's up Gods.. You have been given

the power to create life and also to take life,

how you consider yourself to be anything thing less

then a God, I don't know, with this
tongue I

create lightening, with these hands I
hold rods,

on earth as it is in heaven, so war persist,
Gods

haven't found a way to coexist, when
will the world

acknowledge that we are all one, inter-
connected,

if you cry, I cry, if you smile, I smile, you
die,

I die, you just had amazing sex, I just experienced

that too, There is no separation, no matter what you

do, people spend most there lives pushing it

away but, what you resist persist, my words

peak interest, your soul shake as my words

caress your heart, I'm going to tell someone I

never met before I love them, how's that for a start.

SEPTEMBER

I had a realization today... I am very enlightened yo, I know things for real, I am playing it perfect, at times, I often fail to remember that this isn't real, I work through it perfect still, I am in this dimension fully, I see you pretending not to be reading what I am writing, Peace.

ACCEPTENCE

Thank you, so much, for being here,

in that: padded room,

in that: glass cube,

in that: mental cell,

on that: long rainy

walk to the shelter,

under that bridge,

where I slept.

My nigguhs, I

don't know the meaning

of love. I hate

you all, I wah

see yuh all bawl,

all I do, is destroy everything

around me and brawl.

I am a member of hell

and the devil is my best-ee, (yeah BFF)

my future is written,

my flesh and my soul

are one, married:

no matter how dark,

how cold, I see myself

for who I am, for what I do,

my words: are hollow,

my actions: half-hearted,

my faith: I wish was in me.

I trust myself, I trust

myself to do what I

have always done,

to be how I always been, a soldier

a soulviver, I am a believer.

DECEMBER

It has been a mission still, I am able to maneuver past any of the bullshit this made-up world has thrown at me, Xhena comes out here, I totally fall in love, I am letting every feeling, every thought, everything she is going through affect me, my mood, actions, everything, it's like when it comes to her, it is real, I am giving my self-headaches, I am becoming frustrated and emotional over the way she is feeling, my heart is saying yo, help her, like how you help(ed) yourself, help her, she needs you, put everything on hold and hold her

like no one did for you, my mind is saying, fuck her, this world, and everyone and everything in it, she abandoned me, I knew there would be a time she would need me, as will the rest of them, walk away and let the bitch drown, we are at war with ourselves, it is a lot of us in here, I knew this day would come, choose he(r) or everything else, I am choosing her, I have already made my choice no doubt, I just hope I am mentally ready for this, her, I am ready, I will give it all I got, I got me.

SILENT

Silent tears for the ones I

have left behind, I miss

them, more than my heart

can bare. Is it love or fear

may be both. The sound of daddy

echoes in my soul. When I

had them in possession, I was filled

with holes, there are no longer in my
care

and I am officially whole, I miss

them. Little extensions of me, this false

life can be so real when I want it to be.

MARCH

**What a week, I just called off again,
every two weeks I'm averaging a call**

off, not okay with Me but, then it is. Jr is not coming out here (here to visit me) I realized that it was all talk, as it usually is, when I am supposed to, I will see him again. I have been kind of Irritable this week, letting things get to me very easy, I meditated on it, I am bothered by multiple things, during my (meditation) session I got my answers, I will apply them, at this moment, I do not remember all the answers, that's okay, I have decided to love Cia all out, no matter what, just open my heart totally, last time did not end well but, it was worth it, the experience was priceless. I am ready to give it another shot, lol, this girl is something else. Going to try and get to the college, time is ticking, no worries, decided, that I will take a

little time to enjoy where I am at for a little, I have been tired a lot, sleepy most days. I have been putting a lot of pressure on myself about poetry when there is no need for it, I will relax for a while then, gradually hit It again, I know it will work out per-fectly, thanks for listening.

TEMPTATION

A TALE OF BIPOLR-EE

"I've laid dormant

on the floor

of the abyss,

allowed others to own

the deed to my lands,

allowed comedians to laugh

over my body, hold hands,

Sing and dance,

allowed them to take chunks

of sustenance from my hands.

The anger from the "Take the L" **emote

knocks down the protectors,

agony paralyzes the receptors" by Lion-
BlessUp

"Dear Trouble,

I want to fuck you and you want to fuck
me. I

am already in a great partnership in this lifetime. Rather,

then stay away from you and make this an awkward class.

I have chosen to inform you that you are worth

way more than a sexual look from a married man. I

am writing this letter due to my inability to

successfully turn down sexual advances. (consistently).

So, yeah, leave me alone and I will leave you alone.

You are a breeze of California's Venice
beach

if I ever felt one. I know you have someone

that is really checking for you. Peace🙏

Sincerely, That nigga over there (Tnot)

Temptation.

Ps, let's both do better for the ones that
deserve it."

(moving the cursor over to the send button) Click, (in my head) did I proofread
that? Thank goodness I got

that out, the fire has calmed. First time I
made eye contact with Trouble it wasn't
fireworks. More like a

scene from the websites I would only view using incognito. In the back-ground, heavy drums and

Kid Rock saying something like "Body of a devil and she smells like sex, I can tell your trouble, but I'm still

obsessed". I was hooked on the pain that darkened her contours. My brain lubri-cated at the thought of

racing my fingers north towards Atlanta starting from Miami which is Troubles hairline on the back of her

neck. The titillating feeling, I would get from cupping the middle of her hair with my palms flat, fingers

erected but planned so, only the tips are

in play applying the much-needed pressure to enhance the

transfer of energy. Moving forward
through the brush of confused hair,
down the slope of her forehead

heading south, stopping only when the
fingertips has reached the sensitive spots
on her chin and jawline.

Troubles' neck is now positioned for
mouth to mouth, only her neck is the
true intended target. I look up

and reenact a scene written by Bram
Stroker himself. Most would have
become the texture of putty by now,

but you are fixed on leaving teeth
imprints on my cheeks. I snap out of it,
the sickening feeling and

swelling of my manhood adds to my mental curiosity. (scanning the room panoramically) I am so proud of

myself. I did not make the same choice expecting a different result, finally. I'm the man.

Reaching for loose stationary on my desk, a new message is constructed:

"Dear Closet Freak,

I want to get some alone time with you, and you

would like alone time with me. Unfortunately, I

am in a solid situation that entails things be done

on perfect timing. Here is a list of rules

for the game, should we

decide to play. One; no contact outside

of school. Two; no lingering looks *key

as niggas is observant. Three;

never learn my name. Four; recycled sex

spots are a no-go. *every experience
must be new. Five; no

chemistry is the best chemistry. Six; no

being truthful *lying provokes creativ-
ity. Seven; no

social media contact *includes but, not
limited

to views, likes etc… Eight; unless using
as artistic

expression, never

release the five w's of us. Nine; never
confirm

a meet up *maybe, might, we'll see,
shrugs, I will let you

know, and okay are all acceptable. ten;
during sex

explore all your options. Eleven; only
meet if you want to

meet *no obligations. Twelve; if waiting
at a meet spot

for more than five minutes, leave

*only thing that can come after that is trouble. Thirteen;

communication is done face to face and through handwritten

letters *which, will be given back to the author

upon meeting up. Fourteen; get what you want out of our

experiences as they are temporary. Fifth teen; only sex

is safe sex, prophylactics is a must. If you agree

to the strict side piece code of ethics, then please refer to rule

number nine. Closet freak understand
that if you

agree to these terms, we can never be
more than a side

piece to one another. No friendship, no

association, no truth, no intimacy, no
depth, no love,

and no status, WE JUST FUCKING.

See you around,

Sincerely, That nigga over there (Tnot)
Temptation

Ps, I'm glad about either choice you

make but, I would rather be your
friend."

(lighting a plastic tip cigar) I inhale smoothly and exhale, releasing the smoke slowly making sure to fill

each cloud with all my worries and guilt of what I had just manifested in my per- fectly normal drama free

life. The Thai Chi influenced music keeps chanting "you are protected". I hear more lyrics, but these are the

only words I'm listening to. I pick up the pure colored stationary and admire the softness of my

penmanship. Holding the left and right ends of the stationary I lie down on the opposite side on the desk

with the ends facing me. (smirking face

while nodding head north and south) I match the left and right end

into their corresponding matches making sure the ends line up. Holding the ends in place with thumbs I

place the other four fingers on each hand flat on the stationary together mimicking the hands of a penguin.

Making sure to keep thumbs in place, I massage the air out of the folded stationary lining up all sides

evenly. I follow these folding steps five more times; the finished product favors the sticky notes

(3.8cmx5.1cm) I write important ideas on. I zip open a backpack that has a stitched photograph of a past president with a paper rolled big head at his lips and the number 420 hologram throughout the exterior of

the bag. The whites behind my lips always makes an appearance at the sight of this backpack. (deep

relaxed exhalation) I still cannot believe I have a presidential brother in hemp, hell yeah. I gracefully locate

a fold top sandwich bag (16.5cmx13.9cm), my index card carrier and nestle the letter in between the

hundreds of homemade index cards that come in various unidentifiable shapes. I fold the bag back long

side inside and over the cards. Flip the

start side over the top of the bag. I place gently back in a tight spot

to the back left lower corner of the backpack. Ticklish chills go up my neck distributing the feeling around

my head simultaneously, (in my head) asmr. Walking out the door I take a memory screen shot, the room

looks different, I am different.

The drive to school becomes life changing. Tall leaning trees full of bright greenery. replenishing

breeze circulating through the vehicle clockwise exiting through the dark tented sunroof drawn back a

quarter of the way, just enough for the

breeze to escape. At eighty miles an hour a feeling of saddle bagged

arms around me, fingertips firmly tenderizing the cords that appear at my neck and disappear behind my

ear. I settle into my seat and begin a lite meditation session. Embracing sounds and smells of the Florida

toll roads. Inhale, one two three hold. Exhale, one two three hold. Inhale, one two three hold. Exhale, one

two three hold. Inhale one two three hold. Exhale, one two three hold. *Granpy's light bulb just went off on

top his graduation cap. The pros of having a side piece:

i. Less sexual frustration

ii. The thrill

(side bar thought leading to a song) I've been through this before. It played out the same way with the same

results every time. (in dramatic fashion) "And God asked why? And I reply, for the thrill. Nothing ever

makes me feel this real", the pleasing tone in my ears cause the grip on my eyelids to loosen. One two three

hold. Exhale. (inside head) The Weeknd is that guy bro, on me. (eyes open)

Mr. Do right and Tnot agree to switch seats

(Tnot recites);

> "I aint never had a pimps' hand
>
> But that limp was a muthafucka.
>
> I ain't never had a pimp's hand
>
> But that limp was a muthafucka.
>
> I ain't never had a pimp's hand
>
> But, that limp (pauses for effect)
>
> that limp is a muthafucka."

Arms cross at the chest right going left and left going right. Beads that tastes of Florida tap water with a

stirred in salt tab hungered my taste buds. (talking a loud to self) Bro this is who you are. You need to accept it bro. Straight up bro. You are a player bro, face it, embrace it. This game was designed for you bro,

master it. I know it's lonely in that ocean, but you still must swim it. A player is what you are destined to

be. Remember who is in charge know, Tnot. I get things done. Way back when you wanted that 1992 black

Chevy Tahoe, the ones with the chrome, Brony's on them. I got us that. Back when I had to get us the $450

needed for prom, Tnot baby. I apply the solutions that we speak but, never do. I am your hustle, your drive,

your racing heartbeat before you win.

I park on the top floor of the parking garage. Turn the music up enough to rattle the trunk. right hand

grabs the sun visor from the right side of back seat on the floor. I Get out the car and give the sun my full

attention and reach for it with my arms, imagination, and soul.

(out loud poetical)

Temptation

Ladies giving into Temptation

leads to bad

relations, for to love me

is to

abhor the hate

of the world.

*Granpy is a character from the cartoon (if you know you know).

**emote is from an internet game (if you know you know.

CALM

When I lived divided,

my mind stayed double sided,

because of my light inside, I couldn't hide it,

dam sho couldn't fight it,

you could say, I busted through the nuts

and came through the shaft.

Yup, I'm now that big black nigga

That'll kick yo ass

OR we can sit back and puff

some grass and watch the bullshit

pass.

THEY

They: Tell us what you know.

Me: I don't know anything.

They: I don't believe you, now tell us what we want to know.

They: Karl, take it easy if he gets mad,

we will not be able to control him, whispered Dennis.

They: Fine, bring him down from there and put him in a seat. Now Luanie, you need to listen very carefully. I need you to answer the following; How did you recognize us? When did you know you had the ability to enter people's minds? How are you able the see the world as you do? How did you find out who "THEY" really are?

Me: (Exasperated, still, able to exaggerate my words) I need a cigarette. I don't know the answers to any of the questions you are asking of me. All I can do is offer a story. Take it or leave it, besides death doesn't exist any way.

They: Hey, fuck you, do you have any

idea the shit storm you have caused, what you are doing to this world! Karl bring it down a little, no Dennis I will not. Luanie thinks he knows but, he knows dick. This story better be what we need ass milk, or you're going up by the arms again, that metal hook wants your chains around it.

Me: (Exaggerated breath). Just keep the cigarettes coming. My Afghanistan tour was coming to an end. I was leaving the gym; the climate was still and clear you could see every star in the galaxy in Afghanistan. on my way out of the gym, I met with a guy he was a military contractor. I don't remember his name and really don't want to. He was light skin, kind of banana skinned with the same sprinkle of dark spots all over his face. I say he was about 66 inches tall with a big afro, if I had to guess his age, I'd say 26 or 27. He knew things and carried his self as such, he was the type to listen to people converse about a truth and if he feels they are both wrong, he will not criticize them aloud but in his head saying the nastiest things. We started talking mainly about nothing, surface stuff. we met with another military contractor by the six feet sandbags called *Hesco* barriers in the middle of the camp. I don't recall his name either, just that he stood about 73 inches tall very dark and looked exactly like dude daddy in *He Got Game.* He stood with assurance and spoke as if he watched a hundred speeches on YouTube. At this point the conversation goes somewhere else, still do not know what sparked it, just that it felt uncomfortable like a sudden shift in wind or a change in climate. The taller guy did most of the talking, he said that the bible is a lie, that all the stories of Jesus is untrue and the same with Moses and other supposed prophets. They only tell us this to control us. I wanted to call bullshit right there and then but, I had no friends, so I listened in disgust. But, I listened.

That night I got no sleep which was normal but, I was on the internet looking up everything they had said. I read up on the Sumerian tablets and Babylonian texts. I seen with my own eyes the story of prophets being told repeatedly through the centuries, only difference was the names had been changed. Fear came over me, the kind right before something happens. I seen the taller guy later that month, I brought up the topic and he quieted me and said he was moving to another camp. he gave me his email and a look that I didn't know I knew so well, relief and empathy. I confronted the shorter guy and was given the cold shoulder. I didn't understand, why put this information out and then not want to speak on it? As if they were afraid. Every chance I got until I left Afghanistan, I searched the internet. I tried to share what I was learning with people I felt I could consider family and was met with resistance, no one cared or wanted to hear it.

Back in America for almost a year and things are going great I got a house, wife, almost all my kids, two businesses, and I am in school. I was on my way to class, a lady and some guy she was with stopped by to look at this beat up old A to B car my wife was selling. The lady was speaking to my wife when I came outside, her attention shifted. She was tall, European, curly blonde hair, and very easy to look at, life had been kind to her. I walked past her and kissed my wife goodbye; the lady says to me "You are such a light. You have an aura around you. But you will never burn as bright as you are supposed to unless you get away from the people that hate you. They wish to dim you." She directs my eyes to follow hers and I do, they led to my wife. The fire in my wife's eyes kindled, the smoke coming from her ears smelled of anger. The lady's guy friend says to me "That was $50s worth of information", she hands me a card and said come see her. She was a psychic and she just hit me with a free reading. I thought about her words and actions for many days and nights, I didn't get it. What was I missing? What am I not seeing? What am I not doing? Who are "They"?

As the questions started so did the spiral downward. After I lost everything, I considered important in order to seem successful. I was living with a lover that I strung along for nine years. She was 68 inches tall, caramel complexion with a 90's Olympic style body with a face no one else had. She had an exterior shell fitting for a hell spawn. On the inside, she was charred, a torch that was being prepared, I know one day it will be ready to be ignited. I was in love, and I had nothing but time on my hands. My schedule was to die for, I had sex for about four to six hours during the day and at night I studied books, watched documentaries, and wrote poetry and ideas. One night we were sitting outside as we usually do on the weekends, I observed that she was always looking up at the sky. I asked, how come the interest in the sky? She says to me, "Look up and choose a star, not one blinking or one to bright", I did as she instructed. The image I seen changed my life forever. First, I saw nothing, then in an instant, I saw how fast the earth was spinning, I was compelled to look deeper, then, I saw them. It must have been millions, no billions, even trillions, no this was a number uncountable to humankind. I saw "THEY". My lover reached out her hand to me, I took it, she led me down the stairs of our 2nd floor dwelling and into the middle of the street and says, "see baby you are special, look at your skin its glowing". We spent the next hour which felt like an eternity looking at "THEY". After that night I was different, and my lover did not remember a thing.

Whatever was in me had activated, I was different. Everything around me was different, plants had a different smell, look, and texture. I could feel everything around me. A bug would be killed in front of me, and I would feel how the other bugs felt that was present. I could tap into peoples' minds, mostly involuntary. My lover would be giving me head and I would look into her eyes as she begged for me to cum without saying a word. This was getting insane; I was not able to stop or block any of this. As weeks went on it got more profound, everything wanted me. Everywhere I went people wanted to talk to me and did so, animals whimpered for my touch, bugs crowded the door to my apartment and followed me almost everywhere. I felt like I was losing it, I started meditating hoping to quiet it down some. My lover started despising me and my children and family was beginning to fear me. Everyone started staying away from me, most times I was alone, even when people were around.

I started to receive visions from "THEY". Visions of things that happened in the past, present, and future. I shared my vision with as many people as I could, no one believed me. I felt the world turning on me, hating me for releasing the truth. I would come across people, and they would tell me to stop it, be quiet, keep the information to myself. I refused to listen, my lover would be with me and tell people I am joking and whisper, "stop being fake" in my ear. By this time,

I had embraced the fact that I had been changing and decided that I was going to dedicate myself to helping humanity. I started a foundation (walk for Humanity), walked everywhere and spoke to as many people as possible, and read many books by Authors on how to heal the human species.

One day, I woke up and everyone's thoughts were in my head, I could not even hear mines. My lover sprayed all the bugs in the bathroom killing most of them, I could not fight back the tears. We are on the freeway, and she said what I knew she had been thinking but was hoping she wouldn't say. That it was over, she was moving out. I was devastated, even though, she hated me now and resented me at least she still listened to me and my thoughts. That night I was a wreck, my abilities was at such a high, I refused to calm down. I meditated; in the meditative state, a thought came to me. Don't be mad at the enforcer, be mad at the coward who gave the order. Neo was a problem to the *Matrix* because he became a virus, he disrupted the normal thought pattern of everyone he came across, this is the reason every prophet had to go. I intended on doing the same and you know what, it worked.

They: Dennis, bag him.

MAY

I got real with a lot of things since my last entry, I let people know that I knew something was going on, I told some people exactly what I know, it felt peaceful, releasing it made me

feel instantly better, I found myself allow(ing) a couple of people and things get to me, I know why I am becoming more intertwined with this dimension, this reality knowing I created it excites me, as I know what's around that corner, I am imbedded in poetry and I am creating things to slow my process which is so funny, I am remembering why I love it. See you next week, I still haven't revealed the full story yet, not even to myself.

PERSONALITY QUIZ

In the Dollar Tree, the night before thanksgiving for no reason other than to kill time. Full of business professionals scrambling for last minute seasonal items. Staring at the green beans reminded me of my reality. Thoughts of my home life pinches my lower elbow continuously creating discomfort.

After a strong bump from behind and quick strength check, I turn to my partner and say nothing, she cries. No shift in eye movement and in mouth twitch, I shake my head smirk and walk away. Last year was the same shit. No money for thanksgiving food and no time to go get any. Walking to the bus stop after work was cold and lonely as my ring of shame, only had room for one loser. I want to go to jail. It's what I deserve, and I need some time off, this shit is too much pressure.

ABOUT THE AUTHOR

Luanie Lion BlessUp Lambey-Bermudez

I am a father of six children (maybe 7, I

have a loose Cock), a husband to a loving, intelligent, beautiful wife. I am a poet at heart who uses different mediums to express that poetry. Twelve years of military service has left me with scars that can and cannot be seen. After a severe mental break, homelessness, and years of being in the care of the VA, I was finally able to get back on my feet. I now live on the Left Coast in Sizzle Town. I am a creator of conversation and promoter of personal growth. Over 10 years as an established poet, writer, serial-expressionist, and magazine editor. I completed bachelor's degree at University of Central Florida and currently enrolled in a master's program at University of Nevada, Las Vegas. BlessUp

CHAPTER 3

HYPERMANIA

LUANIE LION BLESSUP LAMBEY-BERMUDEZ

FEAST

A Medicinal spoken word

Inspired by: "I have been simmering in rage and revenge, but I've convinced myself it'll make me taste better in the end"   -NICOLE G-

I just masturbated

and slurped up the contents

from my wrist, hand,

and between my fingers.

For me personally,

the taste was as sweet

as the release. Flashback

to a time when I didn't taste

so sweet, no, it had nothing

to do with what I was eating,

in reality, it did, by this, I

don't mean meat. I simmered

in that revenge and rage

until it burned out, then I

blended the excess. I feed

my spirit delightful things

and now I taste like honey.

JANUARY

Last night was a night to remember, I scream, I felt like I was about to lose it, I felt like I was back in that living room about to take a back seat, I find myself taking pills to sleep, mediation gave me a reality check still, I allowed the feeling of hurt and vengeance taking over me, I allowed it, I wonder how can I get back at her (Xhena) how can I hurt her back, I want to though, I am choosing to though, that's the part that has my eyes watering, This shit is so typical,

I wrote a story that is so predictable, I want to change it, I will change, I will continue to be me, the real me, fuck her and this game, It is not difficult still, I have allowed this jackhammer to beat at my foundation, Xhena is playing her role beautifully, I will play mines even better, I will bend to this fake reality, shit, might even break, no matter what, I can be put back together, stronger then the last.

DON'T FUK WIT ME

Teenage fantasies

keep me in some bullshit,

Don't get outta pocket, I

keep a full clip, I

am loaded with a disrespectful

lip, and a nasty tongue

with fuck you bitch

in between my hips,

you'll be jiggin' like dat bright

nigga from beat it,

reporting all your thoughts

to the pips, they go bring it to they boss, I'm

the biggest ROSS my flow

bends and twist, try not to get lost,

I hope you hearing this in the day,

at night I be unmedicated with the
energy

of Mr. Frost, I often get lost,

but, fuck it, I'll just have to pay

the cost.

MY PRECIOUS

My heart is a ring

that sings to the ladies

by the pool.

The notes

vary, depending on the sun,

this day party hold 3 hun,

whoever hears my song,

is that one.

My heart is a ring

that sings, to the ladies

by the pool. Curiosity

brings them near but, only

the one for me ears

can hear, the rest just stare.

JANUARY

This week was amazing, I don't really remember what happened, let me stop, I'm lying to myself, I got great

news, the apartment I had applied for, accepted me. It's exciting, I didn't think I was going to get it, the man who name is Ben seemed reluctant to say yes, like, he was skeptical about letting me rent the place, it's cool though in the end, he said yes. I have to drop-off my packet this morning, I have a feeling, I am going to be waiting for at least two weeks before I get it back which, okay, I guess everything happens perfect, just the way it's suppose to, is what I keep telling myself, one day I will fully believe it, I'm close. I went to orientation on Wednesday it was a good experience, early that morning, I ran into a girl that I swore gave me syphilis. Turns out, I didn't have syphilis, I had scabies (4rm the shelter I lived at the time) haha, I apologized for blaming her for something she didn't have. We laughed about it, I haven't seen her since that day we fucked in the pool bathroom at the Days inn. That was very very fun, no condom of course, I'm still living life on the edge, haha, not funny though but, it really is. Anyway, we looked into each other's eyes, we held hands, very passionately kissed a couple of times, I know for a fact, she still wants to fuck me, the head was bomb, not better than Lene's but, close enough, I was not happy about her spitting out my leche, not cool. Her Pussy was super tight, I loved it, even tighter than my supposed virgin wife, haha, I let people tell me anything, I don't know if that's (a) good or bad (thing), I don't know, I just don't care enough to dispute their truth. So Yeah, it was good seeing her, I want to fuck her again too so, the feeling is mutual. At orientation, I saw this Very young Haitian girl I met her before the week before, when I went to get my badge, I could tell she was into me as she sat down right next to me when they were tons of empty seats, worked out great because, I sat down next to this light skin cutie, I was working on her but, not to hard, really, I was trying to create a connection, even though I know better but hey, doesn't hurt to try any way, we hit it off right away, me and the Haitian girl, I even had to move seats and she still followed me, haha, she really likes me. When I saw her at orientation, I was going to say hi (but) when I spotted this red bone sitting across from her, baby girl was bussing, long hair and slim, just like I like them. I had to do something to stand out so I hugged the Haitian girl, her name is Miley by the way, so I hugged her so tight it took Miley's breath away and definitely got the redbones attention, since she was looking, I introduced myself, she wasn't interested but, she was very intrigued. I sat next to her in the classroom, and I could feel Miley's eyes on me the whole time. Lunch came, Miley was on me hard, I did not want what she was getting so, got pizza, the redbone was sitting by herself and so was Miley, I was on the fence for a minute then, something felt right about sitting with Miley, I pulled a last-minute attempt by telling her I was going to sit somewhere else, she followed. We had our first real conversation I was still preoccupied with looking at old girl but that went away when Miley told me she was in college and that she was in school to become a physical therapist assistant, for the first time (during) lunch, I knew I chose right, later, I found out that the red bone is only seventeen and I'm on probation so, yeah, no, no. Next time, I see Miley I am going to make a move, I like her, she is very cute, tall, and soft spoken, also, intelligent, the wig she wears is funny, I accept it yet, I will address it in the future. Lately, I have been realizing a lot (of) things about myself and the everything around me, in short, none of this shit is REAL! Thanks for listening until next week, oh

yeah, I might like football again peace.

CLOSER

I am hurting, I

am dying on the inside, I

cant even explain to myself,

why the truth is demoralizing

enough to put me back behind bars,

tears running down my face like cars

at the autobahn, high speed, I

seriously need help from the god

that is inside me, all these truths

is starting to divide me. No,

not again, please, not again,

last time was so bad, it took 16

months to get out of that, as a matter

of fact, I am still in it. The day I

realized the truth, I tried to turn

back but the path behind me,

had been erased. I am everything

they fear, the secretive whispers, I

hear, I am a dragon with no leer,

a Lion with no pride, to myself, is who I

confide. On my own roller coaster, I'm

going for an emotional ride, ups

and downs, extreme highs and danger-
ous

lows, I keep telling myself you can han-
dle

this bros. They are trying so hard to
make

me care and I am too numb, still, the
truth

is here, how can I care, is there such a
thing

as being too aware, not being able to
perform

is my new fear, what will they do if people

stop watching? How would the show

be? Through, I feel mentally incapable,
low key

I want to be through, done with it, the
stench

of failure haunts my nose like hidden
underwear

full of poo, I am going to blow the whistle,

the feeling I carry is so bad, what else can
they

do? The worst has been done, kill

ME? Then what? I always come back,

make the world hate me? To late already

accomplished, soon the world will know

what I know and pretend like they just heard

for the first time, pretend they will, don't

matter, I am dropping the first dime.

JULY

**What am I doing dealing with her.......
How could (you) low(er) your feelings to hurt when the way she felt
was never real, have you ever met
anyone who doesn't go back to the
thing they said they would never go
back to.... Not even, I still carry conversation with the women who is
responsible for this whole thing,
how I care, how come, she is only**

doing it for affect, she is only still with you to make you pay for breaking her heart.... She hurt and she wants you to feel the same way she feels, pay attention to what and how she is doing it, feel the hurt, allow her to feel good about what she did, she finally got to you, she won but, not really.

RELEASE

Slow and smooth, steady and fast,

just don't stop, keep running, even if you

have to come to a shuffle. It's getting

more difficult to suppress these truths,

the things I see, the decisions I make,

is all in line with the course my life. Look,

look at my words, for reasons well known, I

often dislike me, my eyes entice me,

which way do I go, any direction holds

an experience. No such thing as good or bad,

happy or sad, joy or being mad. My niggas, I

am glad I woke up to this the journey. I realize

being yo self is a costly one, fudge it, I am considered

the bossy one, the glossy one, the flossy one, you

my friend, can call me the saucy one. I know my path

its an easy one; enhancing the game

that was given to me by updating the old

ones. (sidebar) my soul keeps crying so let me

say this "I LOVE DICK" at least I did when I

wrote this. Naw, let me stop the "HIP-BAIT". I get chedda

now, I live betta now, me gyal dah wah go go get-ah now.

Hate-ah's are mad, I mastered this, go against

me, I won't raise a fist, your mortal mind

can't hurt this soul, its mines. Imma float before anyone

do. (side bar) men and women impress me, when I

don't release my soul, it stresses me, I got more goals

then Mr Gretzky, (side bar) youngin' what the hell

is you watching? My goals, I write them down

and achieve um. Thank you so much beloved

for making me great, allowing me to move past

and embrace the hate, for making me realize my

truth, the sweat on my face shows that I am close

to you, you continue to give me everything I

ask for, thank you. In my name I pray, amen.

JANUARY

I'm so late, lol but better than never this week was amazing I have been having so much fun these women I work with really like me. I have been asked if I am gay twice already

that's code phrase for, "your too cute you must be gay". I haven't decided who I am going to have sex with or if I am, I'm kind of thinking about just leaving me as a fantasy right Now, let them aspire to have sex with me. I like the attention I know that we will see I am just going to play it real chill I choose to have a Valentine but who will be the lucky winner Haha speaking of vain, Xhena and I are officially done speaking she told me how she felt which I truly feel was due to whatever she has going on in Las Vegas just could not bring herself to tell me the real reason the truth will come out one day I know that much. I know it's for the better as I was allowing her to become my excuse my distraction so it really worked OUT for me I love it. I had sex on Tuesday I had an absolute blast guess what she swallowed yes her vagina was huge Lol I liked it she was super wet, the best part was when I was done saying my poem in her ear baby girl was crying wow NOW that was a top ten moment. The next day she told me she was falling for me I told (her) I would catch her I think that response hurt her feelings as she decided to tell me about the other guy lol that really likes her so that was probably the last time we will have had sex which is fine it was so much fun what more can you ask for amazing head great Sex yes. I am already seeing results from my workout plan then again I have been going hard I like it though my balance is amazing I wonder how will it change when I move will it slow down intensify. I can't wait but I am lol the house is so enjoyable drama all the time never dull I am going to miss it I already do. I have been meeting a lot of interesting people lately I like meeting new people I hope the bright girl from Ireland emails me straight up if she does I'm out there B. Yo I did my poem for Noel and friends you should have seen their faces priceless I love poetry, I entered in an art festival at the VA I know I submitted three masterpieces win or lose in societies eyes in my eyes I already won the minute I decided to take that leap I won and that's real. I am excited to perform it I am going to blow them away I know that. Until next time thanks for listening peace.

REALIZATION

Everybody wants me,

My light haunts me,

everywhere I go, I take myself with me.

I look in the mirror and I see the same
hater,

how can I get away from myself, running

does no good, I'm always right there, I

tell myself, to give me some space, let me

breathe, gosh, hit me wit some time

to think. I don't want to juggle multiple

women playing Russian roulette with
my penis,

Unprotected sex leads to three things; one

you could have a baby, two you can contract

a disease, three none of thee above knowing

full well sooner or later I'm going to have to deal

with either option one or two shit maybe both. I

took an oath, that the old me is dead yet, I

am still willing to miss out on a job

for the opportunity to score some head,

take a skeez-ah to bed. I choose not to lie

and still, I tell lies for this game

that I feel I have to play, fuck this game,

yes, this one, it's a shame I like to play

it tho. I feel like I am something different,

the script says I must remain the same;

Hate the ones that crossed me, manipu-
late

them and extract revenge, carry a chip

on my shoulder -n- go farther than they

ever thought possible, just so I can see

their face, as the one they turned their backs

on, made it to see another day. I

erased your bullshit teachings I found

a greater way. Honestly that sounds like

so much fun, great for dramatic television,

I really don't care about nothing or no one, I

only think about me, nothing you do offends

me, I don't take anything seriously, I

just want to be me. Not in this LIFE,

the bosses say, maybe in the next, I

am going to bed more women

make more babies, create more drama,

and break more hearts, I guess it's time

for me to start playing my part.

APRIL

Feeling a little down, not as much as I was, naw, no lie, I really miss Cia it hasn't even been a full week, I have contacted her, told her I missed her, yes, I put myself out there, I keep telling myself they set this up on purpose, that I should not care, as it is fake anyway, yet, she is all I think about, had a conversation with Xhena and all I can think about is Cia, I got it bad. I am paying great

attention to my environment without trying, my medication is not working anymore, my senses are coming back even stronger, I have chosen to embrace it, no more fighting, no matter the worldly consequences, the joy I have in me is meaningful, my mind is free, I accept that. My new reality scares and shock me, as I realize there is no reality nothing is true so many lifetimes of lies how can one find truth then again what is the real meaning of truth thanks for (the) listen, worldly, I am doing excellent progressing I wonder if they know I know if they do what are they waiting for then again what am I waiting for.

HUMANITY

(alone in a crowded world.)

Thank you, so much, for being here,

In that: padded room at da bottom of 33rd

In that: glass cube at the top of 33rd

In that: mental cell at the Treasure Coast Forensic center

On that; long rainy walk to the shelter,

where they denied me a bed, under

that bridge by the stadium, where I

slept. You nigguhs, do not know

the meaning of love, beloved, I hate

them all, I wah see dem all bawl,

all they do, is destroy everything around

them and brawl. I am a member of hell

and the Devil's my best-e, yeah BFF.

My future: is written in blood,

my flesh and my soul are one, married,

no matter how dark, how cold, I see

you nigguhs for who you

are, for what you is, your words:

are hollow, your actions:

halfhearted, my faith: is in me.

Trust you, I trust you to do what you

have always done, to be how you

have always been.

FLIPHOLE

Dear Lion,

when you first bought me, I could sense your excitement when you removed me from the shelf. I

was so nervous because you had picked me up several times before. You just looked at me and inspected

every detail, then you would set me down and leave. Finally, you bought me and brought me to my new

home. I sat patiently and watched you

read my instructions, at that moment, I knew this was going to be a

lasting bond. That night you took such precaution. You opened me up, ran your hand softly on my insides,

tingling me in every way. You were so gentle Lion, you respected the fact that this was my first time.

Remember, I was so wet for you. We made love three times that night, wow, I fell in love. As time went on

things got better, I was so happy. Not that I am not happy now, just concerned. You no longer take your

time with me; very rarely do you take the time to clean me anymore. Things have changed between us and

I truly desire for the old you back. If not, just know that I am still here, and I still love you. I will continue to

give you my all. Thank you for listening, I hope you do not take this the wrong way.

Love always your favorite red flip hole,

Susie (SUZEE).

SUZEE (SUSIE)

I want you when no one

else does, I give the best

part of you love, Red, because blood

excites you, my makers'

name rhymes with your white

friends' favorite family game,

"JENGA"

I want you when no one

else does, I give the best

part of you love, I watch you

watching me, you desire me

guilefully, you move quick

in my presence, *slow down,*

(-n- remember) I want you when no one

else does, I give the best

part of you love, I am filled

with space channels, overlapping

ripples, thirty-nine textures across

eight intersections, softness that's three

waves deep. I weep, cause I

want you when no one

else does, I give the best

part of you love.

4 DAT COOCHIE

I used to

play games 4 dat coochie,

blow jane 4 dat coochie,

go insane 4 dat coochie,

wear rings 4 dat coochie,

pull strings 4 dat coochie,

spend change 4 dat coochie,

roc chains 4 dat coochie,

drive up to 10 miles.

Yo, I sang 4 dat coochie,

talked strange 4 dat coochie,

sought fame 4 dat coochie.

Kissed an ugly girl

on her lips, I took

trips 4 dat coochie,

gave up grips 4 dat coochie,

get a thousand ones, ya, I

tipped 4 dat coochie,

went hard for the cash.

Yo, I Bought dat coochie bags,

went to jail 4 dat coochie,

in a cell 4 dat coochie,

went to hell 4 dat coochie,

every day I told a lie,

everyhing I did was 4,

dat COOCHIE.

ABOUT THE AUTHOR

Luanie Lion BlessUp Lambey-Bermudez

I am a father of six children (maybe 7, I

have a loose Cock), a husband to a loving, intelligent, beautiful wife. I am a poet at heart who uses different mediums to express that poetry. Twelve years of military service has left me with scars that can and cannot be seen. After a severe mental break, homelessness, and years of being in the care of the VA, I was finally able to get back on my feet. I now live on the Left Coast in Sizzle Town. I am a creator of conversation and promoter of personal growth. Over 10 years as an established poet, writer, serial-expressionist, and magazine editor. I completed bachelor's degree at University of Central Florida and currently enrolled in a master's program at University of Nevada, Las Vegas. BlessUp

CHAPTER 4

MEDICATED

LUANIE LION BLESSUP LAMBEY-BERMUDEZ

DAILY

How do I feel;

Used and abused,

Manipulated,

Strategically moved,

Somehow, I still groove.

JULY

I have gotten upset twice this week, I handled it well, I did not meditate or remind myself this is a false reality, I just felt the feeling and let it pass which, was very, I am going to wake up each day (and) remind myself (o)f the game and how much fun it is to play it, Thanks for listening.

MENTAL SPACE

Monitored well,

firewall blazin' hell,

encryption 2 swell.

MAY

Something happened to me, I feel it, I

know it, things have changed, I am on the perfect pace to win this race, truth was revealed to me in a way only I could understand, I knew the answers and I released them, I know what happened to me that night on the days and months that I was gone (and) checked out, I am looking at them telling them I know, I am over the fear, I wrote my first real poem, told Cia about it, I heard her silently rejoice, weight gone, freedom stepped in (and) my soul took a breather, thanks for listening, I know what happens next.

EASY GOING

Is how I feel,

I'm finally starting to know

the real, what you see is not

what you see,

that's what was told to me,

then what do I see.

(BTW) What's real to me? Your actions,

what you doing, I'm sick

of your inability to do

what your mouth says your

doing.

Is it real? I mean really, is it?

This thing that I'm pursuing,

reach for the stars forget

that, I'm reaching for the sun,

so what if it burns so good, I

bet I'm not the only one, if I

am, so be it, I'm plenty, I

not only wish I could, I see

I could, I know I could,

soon, I will begin to levitate, I

already do it in my dreams,

during my meditation session I'm

bursting through the clouds, spinning

in circles, secretly racing a Russian jet,

don't ask questions you know the answer

too, of course I won. I am America's best

kept secret, just you wait and see,

the best thing like a cold glass of iced

tea (valerian) in the middle of a southern

summer, I'm training day and night

with little distractions,

I have created a healthy balance,

who you know been right-handed

for thirty years and now super eloquent

with the left, news flash, I wrote

this with the left, Yes, baby, my right

brain creating, baby, while my left

brain, keep thinking, baby, shout

out to brain gym. Cut out the flesh,

sugar, smoking, and the drinking, I

not only want to live, I want

to live amazingly, I cleaned out

my temple, starting from the inside,

as you can tell, I finished polishing

the outside, now I shine like a diamond

and yes, I'll last forever.

To the ones that hate me, THANKS

#haterstandup, to my frenemies, stick

around, you'll graduate to a hater

soon enough, I will be at your ceremony,

helping you along by conquering

every obstacle that comes my

way. You will not stop me! I

will succeed. I say again, I'm

easy going and that's how I

feel.

-PEACE-

JUNE

I have been missing my children,

imaginary children, I know soon we will be together, it is my time right now and here on out no one else , I know this is a false reality so, I push for things to happen my way, I chose to stay, I know I know how come I chose to stay, just choosing not to remember at the moment still, I am on the path, I feel it, I know it, I am starting to love this life tho, everything is happening my way, never knew I had so much control, that all I had to do is say it. My wish is my command, my confidence is building my soul, goal(s) are being fulfilled, my earthly goals have already been met, Thanks for listening I have been allowing people in this realm of imagination to get to me and I know why.

MEDICATED

The play is cray,

her tat on her pussy,

say slay, beat them drums

harder than Dre, tell them scary

dudes get out da way, between

yo legs, I do not play, professional

player, focused, #24 in dat pussy,

just make sure you pay what you

weigh, got a month of bills stashed

away, it was baked yesterday, it's mash

today, men it's that time time fa drop

ah rhyme, then go lay down and
squeeze

pon me gyal behind, it's not big, butt,

it's mind, not really sleepy tho, but, its
time.

FEBRUARY

Amazing week truly has been an amazing week, I officially moved in Thursday, I didn't have furniture yet so, I used my three (black heavy duty trash bags filled with my belongings) bags as my couch and bed. I feel free, so free, I cried that night, joyful tears, fearful tears, agonizing tears, then, I went for a run, I was so nervous, I had to vomit all I ate all on the sidewalk, pieces of tuna sand-

wich, oatmeal pie, twix, and Diet Coke were everywhere, haha, I felt better after. Friday, I got furniture, it amazing, I picked the perfect stuff, wow, the lady and the staff that helped me were (a) big help. I was looking forward to meeting with Cia just as much as I was looking forward to moving. I love this girl, I really do, she has me, I haven't told her yet, fear, haha, I will next time we meet, I know she feels it, I feel her, I get her, it really seems like she gets me, we talk about everything, I love it, the openness, it's mind clouding for me, when she is around, I forget my reality the truths that I have become aware of, takes a backseat, I was so blown away at dinner, let me keep it, real baby girl was running for the bus (inna) yellow dress, no bra, (no) panties, that said its yours Lion, our conversation was unmatched, we cover topics no one else wants to speak on. I did not want the night to end, I had to find a way to get her next to me in the bed. I am tired, going to bed, thank you for listening.

POETRY

Today has been a trying one,

It's hot af outside

So, it's also a frying one,

This is Lion sun.

DECEMBER

I have Identified multiple issues well, things that have caused some kind of uncomfortable feeling from within, I know that this is not real, this I know with all of me, I still understand that it is possible to walk on but lines of believing and not believing, the battle comes from liking the non-reality too much, so much so that I will start to lose who I truly am again and that is scary, I love who I am even as I pretend to be someone else here, I enjoy this game of pretend and all the stress that comes with it, the fact that I can be whoever I say I am is astonishing, the crazy part is that I am finding myself becoming stressed over sharing this knowledge with people who

knows this already, due to their script they pretend not to.

TRUAMA

I still cry when I

think about living

in the streets,

I feel like these words

should be put

wit some beats.

AUGUST

I am fully imbedded in this world, no escaping, I understand that and with that understanding I know that this

world is mind, I often misplace that reality and play into their reality still, I am in my own world, mostly, do not want to be here yet, now a days I feel like I am choosing to be here, I know how come too, I just refuse to share with myself at the moment, I see what's real,Thanks for listening.

2 MILLIGRAMS OF RISPERADONE

Alone,

I sit silent,

observing conversations;

The laughs start off timid,

sort of unnatural, as the wine

flows, more smiles grow,

bodies start convulsing, mouths

start opening (teeth showing),

and heads start to sway.

Alone,

I sit in silence,

observing people have conversations;

A woman paying attention

to the door, while her guy

friend speaks (there's no connection),

the man feels the weather

and reaches out across

the table, the attempt failed,

his mood doesn't change,

just uses his non dominate

hand, to train his waves

with an imaginary brush,

"Yeah, that's right, brush

that weak ass fade", was the womans,

demeanor.

When I'm alone,

I be silent,

N observe conversations.

PKA LyingTongue Vol.2

JANUARY

Well it's Sunday so, I'm journaling, just had a meeting with Mackie my counselor, she really put things in a different light. I haven't really been looking at this apartment thing with a wide view, I have had (a) kind of tunnel vision. It's a restart, I decide who I keep in my circle and who I don't, so far so good yet, when it comes to the apartment, I have been thinking who can I bring their, which was my past way of thinking of it, I know where that got me, this time I am choosing to take a differ-ent route, I don't know if it will lead to a so called unhappy outcome but, I do know it will be a different out-come. I am going to treat it like a hideout, no one should know where it is, easy, I will really check out potentials, be cautious more than that, I have to be assertive about what it is that I want, that's how I let Danice get (me), not speaking up, lol, Lion not having it. This week was cool this girl Monique gave me her number, she wants to be the first to have sex with me (in my new spot), I want some head, I know she likes to keep secret(s) but, after thinking about It, I choose to be cool, continue to let things play out, I decided to ask myself out for Valentine's day, it's going to be a great time, seafood dinner, before that, I'm going to (the) fun stop, I don't know what it's called but, I am going to get on it. This week has been okay still, doing a lot of flirting with the women I work with, lol, that's always fun. I ran into a girl that I should be afraid of, she gives me this feeling (of) forgetting everything I am doing and doing what she (is) doing, it's crazy, very familiar to me, a lot of her views are different, I really like that about her, she seems fearless, that drive(s) my hormones insane. Thanks for listening until next week.

PURPOSE

I am getting there I swear, I

cleanse out peoples' insides

like a pear, you can hide

what's inside of you, these

words, will rip it out

of you, my tongues a spear,

my soul is the stick, verbal

SHAKA, not Zulu but live through

years of bloodshed, passion

for myself, makes me see red,

my brain has a name for them, I

constantly see dead. The dead

lies dormant inside you, awaken

it, that's the instructions from my

soul, I cut at it with a Hachette,

this happens with ease, I

am a knowle, This dudes a wierdo,

no one laughs this much, he must be

on drugs, no one's this happy, I want

what he has, I am tired of feeling

crappy, the lies we tell ourselves, do you

really believe it? Success can you

really achieve it? The map is given

to me, I find a way to misread it. One

of my strengths is empathy, I

understand your pain, I can feel

your misery, I sense your insecurities,

all your moves says, "self-hate". All I

have come to do is start the debate,

start a conversation, not between me

and you but between me and myself.

Question everything and accept my

inner answers, that's my truths, no

one else's, whatever I choose not

to confront in an unaware crack

it nestles, slowly digging away at my

foundation, scraping away the truths,

morals, and love that I have mortared

together to build this lavish house. I

know from experience, many lives I've

lived, many lives I am managing

right now, at this very moment, helping

others is helping myself as we are one. I

am getting there I swear.

MAY

I was reading when I came across it. Clear as day what I already knew what I had been saying to myself for a while, I am the writer of my own story, that everything that is, Is because of me, I am the architect, I created this world with that being said, everyone and everything works around me, I have opposition that I have created no enemies no villains only people following my instructions, I wrote each and every program, I am a genius, I can have

whatever I choose to have, be where ever I choose to be, do whatever I choose to do, Nothing or no one can stop me only me, I have learned to work with me, be best friends with me, we are married, I am unstoppable! Thanks for listening.

BUSPIRONE

I am afraid, so scared I cry,

death is near, death is here, I

know you, all of you, I

have seen you be4, interacted

with you b4, you have nothing

new for me to explore, how dare

you say you love me, and still,

play this game of pretend,

On the inside, you fug-lee, you

are not who you say you are, I

don't know your true name, so I

call you enemy, you stay close

to me, unable to kill me, I am your

captive, you prefer the synonym guest, I

will not die for you , any of you, I

am so done playing your game,

this whole thing is fake, my girl, my

life, my children, my success, this is all

one big show. Fear has you, fear has me

too. If I am reading this aloud

then that relationship has ceased, I

have seen, how far they will go, to keep

this going. I know you don't pretend out

of your own free will, they put you

through so much, you feel you

can never be yourself, I am ready

to die, my whole life is a lie,

its all made up, what a cruel joke

most say but, all play a role.

To be exact, I see things as they

are, wishing I could rewind

to what they were. To stop marrying

unknowns, I had to first marry

myself, this is me, I am the greatest

poet, the greatest me, and I'm still

scare- ree.

JANUARY

I changed the chapter, the feeling of this world is amazing, I know it's fake still, the feeling is real at least in my brain it feels real, like a VR game, I broke her heart and I don't feel any remorse, that what doing what you feel leaves you with, no regret, no remorse, no thought of

how it affected anyone, this world and all others are mines, last year was epic and very calm and manageable, this year I am taking on more, really, it's the same as I released some things to the breeze. New movements, haha, a glut for trouble, no, addicted to growth.

RUB DOWN

Sometimes the wrong things are natural,

Sometimes the natural, isn't the wrong thing,

school work yes, I have plenty, bills, I

have plenty, money, I have plenty,

Nothing gets done says society,

my spirit is illuminating rays of light,

bills, auto pay, money, auto stash,

schoolwork done at school,

the touches seep dopamine.

OCTOBER

At first, I took the time out to really see, what the reason for them putting this person back in my life, I don't know if I received the answer then, as a matter of fact, I know I didn't, it's a sick game, still, it is my game I forget that sometimes, I realize I let her back in for more reasons than love, Xhena is testing my

patience every day, pushing my teachings to the popping point, (I'm) learning how to be assertive, putting "not sweating the small stuff", to the test, need lees to say, an hour I realize the biggest reason, to start at ground zero with building the team that I need to accomplish something bigger but yet, not more important than anyone (me).

This quest to world peace is going to be a problem, I am God and so I am built with infinite life so, it is my will so shall it be, I know what I must do, I just don't want to lose her but, if I don't then I fear I will loss myself.

MASK

A Golden E-tool

by

Lion BlessUp

taken from

"The Mask" by May Angelou

I laugh to conceal my feels'. They

love to serve me dem pills. I Laugh,

hopin' tears don't become real. To

keep this veterans' banana, inside da
peel. A smile, to Conceal

nineteen months of aggressive therapy,
twice a day at Their

facilities but, look, now, I chill. I laugh to conceal my Crying.

FEBRUARY

Amazing week, I got a lot done, I learned so much about myself, highlight of the week, Jr. (oldest son) found me, wow, he really missed me, I can feel it. We have spoken every day since then, he has matured so much, I wonder what he looks like now, bet he is tall and Fat, his mom always kept him fed well. I am supposed to see him in March, (I'm) kind of nervous but mostly excited, I have gotten real close with Macarra from work, the girl has a partner yet, I know, I am always on her mind, mainly because she is on mine, lol, we made plans to hang out at the opera, we will see. Monique (cutie from work) offered to twist my hair for me, I'm skeptical but, I am going to see where it goes. I hung out with Larrissa at the mall, we had a blast, found out a lot about her, we pretty good, work was cool, I am working on what is my motivation for working there, once my claim goes through what is going to keep me working? It's almost time to leave the shelter, I'm going to miss it. At the park waiting for Cia, we are going fishing today, this is going to be crazy. Thanks for listening.

HEADACHE

Mind is going, refusing to stop, in reality, I

don't want it to, ingenious ideas keep
mashing through,

what shall I do? Who knew I could be so
great,

just eat once a day but, I swear my soul

keeps gaining weight. Oh my God,

who can stop my mental obesity.

(my)Thoughts go here, then thoughts

go there, no lie, my thoughts are every

where, I call them godly thoughts.

My head hurts, until I stop the music,

open word, and start to write to my

own tune, my skills inflate like a balloon

with each poem that is written, I'm

still low key motivated by the kitten.

Keeping my eyes and ears open, peeled,

on a new genre of women, no disrespect

to the shawties I talk to now, I'm

on my mission for something deeper.

I choose to converse about the things

no one wants to speak on, I partake

in the things many shy away from, I

lived my life for the thrills but, my

actions were superficial, shallow, I

played with women's emotions

that wanted them played with

and called it fun, I promise it was easy

any way that journey is done. I'm

into something harder now, stronger;

I stop settling for less, I demanded

the best not of other people, can't control

them, the best from me by me, it left me
feeling

like I'm out to sea all by my lonely, only I

realize I'm not a lone, I have the best

friend I could ever have, myself,

there can and will never be anyone else,

I treat myself like pelt, with the utmost

care and respect, been swimming for long

time, (with) still no land in sight,

the waves have calm, all but the one

I'm riding on, to shore I go.

Want my undivided, listen very care-fully,

you have to go below, not below the belt,

that sensation only last but for so long.

Have to make sure my EGO doesn't Ease

the God Out of me, cockiness

remain healthy tho, soon I'll be wealthy

tho, I know only then they will come

a running, tryna get it any way they

can, sure playing nice at first, the first

no will bring the dirt, out with the stained

underwear, oh, you thought it was hidden,

the shit has been found, transparency

for me is a personal key, nothing anyone

could, would do, will not be taking personally,

I had a chance to end the game, instead,

I decided to play it, see it to the end.

JANUARY

I said, I was going to start keeping a journal at beginning of this year. Here it is the 8th, I am finally making my first entry. I originally thought I would be doing this before bed every day. I decided, I am going to start at (journaling) once a week, at any time. This first week have (has) been very productive, I got a job which, is awesome. My first day haven't been made clear but, my orientation starts on Wednesday 9-4. I am excited, haven't had a real job in over three years maybe more. Scary, really, when I think about it, I know I'm ready to work again. I still don't know how come I waited so long but, I am joyful that I have remembered why I am doing this, I was so lost, gone in the head. It was a crazy time for me, I forgot that this is pretend. I forgot who I really was, pretending not to be pretending can be tricky. The hard part now, is learning how to pretend again without forgetting that I am pretending. I get better every day taking it slow, most days I don't know what I am supposed to be doing so, I always end up doing what I feel I am supposed to be doing (pull ups, planks (high, low), push ups (diamond, close, standard, wide), running for time (2 (got hella far) hrs. I feel like I have no way to release my true feelings so, I decided that this way is the best way even if they are monitoring it. I can release and no one will be affected. I hope the guy Ben (landlord) calls me soon and tells me great news, I am looking forward to moving out, living alone again. (I) have not had that feeling of independence since 2003. I am going to video chat with Xhena (Xhena has the complexion of a tootsie roll, a build like "flo jo" of the 90's, and 68' tall) maybe I type more later thanks for listening.

ABOUT THE AUTHOR

Luanie   Lion   BlessUp   Lambey-
Bermudez

I am a father of six children (maybe 7, I

have a loose Cock), a husband to a loving, intelligent, beautiful wife. I am a poet at heart who uses different mediums to express that poetry. Twelve years of military service has left me with scars that can and cannot be seen. After a severe mental break, homelessness, and years of being in the care of the VA, I was finally able to get back on my feet. I now live on the Left Coast in Sizzle Town. I am a creator of conversation and promoter of personal growth. Over 10 years as an established poet, writer, serial-expressionist, and magazine editor. I completed bachelor's degree at University of Central Florida and currently enrolled in a master's program at University of Nevada, Las Vegas. BlessUp

CHAPTER 5

PEACE

LUANIE LION BLESSUP LAMBEY-BERMUDEZ

TO WHOM THIS MAY CONCERN,

I LUANIE LION BLESSUP LAMBEY-BERMUDEZ WILL BE LEAVING THE HUD VASH PROGRAM AND MY SUBSIDIZED UNIT EFFECTIVE APRIL 30, 2021.

APRIL

I am appreciating my life in the realm and or universe I'm in I have seen

the benefits of my family. I Know I am never alone as I always will have myself, but I will be damned if my family is not my world. They are so essential to my mental health, world, and everything in it. I thank God for all the souls that I have had the honor of learning from. I love life and all its rollercoaster rides, Peace, Thank you God.

REAL SPIT

Why you tryna fold me

by playing me like the old me

I don't drink no more

cruise the street for whores

take rando's on Lake Tahoe tours

stay up all night with a brown skin

cutie and thangs with no goals

so, why you tryna fold me.

JANUARY

I let Danice push my buttons, I was super upset (with her) already, I responded in a way that lets me know, I still have work to do so, it's okay she wants me back there so, I can fall into their cycle of (doing) nothing with my life, just living for everyone but me, not going to happen, almost did, I'm sticking to my guns, this is where I belong. I enjoyed our conversation though, she shared her opinion, a (lot) of her opinion I liked, that (shows) I guess,

we all have grown, she is definitely still mad at me. Thanks for listening, I needed this. Peace.

SATURDAY THERAPY

Today has been slow

took a walk

and worked

on a perfected

flow, focused

on killing

These roaches (competition)

Friend-a-me's

call me Joe

causing mad

death, they go

put me on the Row

speaking of GO

ya'll know

I go in, Like Joker

I gotta twisted

grin, Silently changing

the game Jeremy Lin

put my culture

in every scene

call me Fin

A, Yoda dat Go Paul

And punch, All opponents

against the wall

I'm the type, To hit the mall

with a wooden

box, strong enough to stand

on, with a Mr. Mackey-phe

under my right

arm, "yo, listen

I gotta plan",

in the middle

is where I post

jump on the stage

and lift my shoulders tall

put the bullhorn to my lips

"attention is what I need from ya'll

nowadays, its to easy to fall

repeating the errors

of a forgotten past,

whats your plan to last?

Mines is with this pen

when I write, I have a blast

I'm here to give inspiration to all

your higher, speaking to you

answer the call, visit

https://www.luanies.com/

subscribe to me, then become a patreon

at https://www.patreon.com/Ltmaster-
poet

I'm dope and you know it,"

Cut off the horn

then scoop up my box

and kick rocks

back from my walk

the days still slow

only difference is, I came back

with a glow, Look, it's after twelve

I gotta GO,

Peace and blessings, BlessUp Lion.

MARCH

This week was the best, before I recap the week, all that's on my mind is Cia, I miss her already so soon, I have been texting her more than usual, I knew I would miss her But, not this much, I decided to wash my sheets, the faster I get Her out of my system, the better, I don't think I will see her again, just a feeling I have, you talk about perfect for me I guess that's why to (way too) perfect, I don't know what (who) They plan on me being with but, it is starting to seem that it's not the ones I really want, I keep getting samples of perfection, is that what life is, a bunch of samples, I say that because, nothing last forever. Cia will soon be replaced but, by who, she set the bar high for the next girl, she was everything I wanted to experience in a woman and relationship. Xhena tried to push my buttons with insults, I hope she will get it, I don't care what she says, does, even her so, peace, lol, I kissed Mily (a classmate) on her neck, I felt her vagina throb with juices. I started recording my poems, it's slow motion with my poetry right now, I will pick it up. The goal is clear, do what I have to do to blow, I'm ready, I know it time to unleash what's really inside me, the world has been patiently waiting. I am going to memorize the ones I have written (-N-) perform them. Then when the time is right unleash. I got my card (bank), I'm excited and worried at the same time, I have already planned out most of it (money), I'm still going to work, there's a sign of growth, a lot of trying thing(s) have been happening, I'm very proud of me, my actions have been beautiful, growing getting myself together, King and I having wonderful conversations, (I) haven't worked out much this week, taking a little break, back at it Monday, Larrisa will be coming by to take pictures of me to send to the agencies that I found, something will pop, I feel it, no more holding back, let's go, King has a YouTube

channel, it inspired me. Thanks for listening.

UNAFRAID

2313 is the time I

usually make love

to myself, tonight, my vehicle

to nirvana is words,

I don't feel like writing

but, low key

I do, I promise to love

God, work on my craft,

and keep living, poetry is truth

these words are from deep

beneath my subcutaneous

skin, my thoughts I

apply topically,

ancestral whispers I

express philosophically.

CHECKBOXES

– smoke

– watch porn

– masturbate

– poetry

- read

- write

- Dou lingo

- talk to wifey

- talk with Nunu

- talk to Idara

- play with family

- watch SportsCenter and news

- drive to work and home

- check my account

- check investments

– talk to moms and pops

– walk

– listen to music

– work

– kiss kids goodnight

– give wifey this Wowla

– sing

– rap

– laugh

– love

– take meds

– think of ideas

– sleep

RECOGNIZE

I'm living my blessed life

A full of stress life

A relaxed life

Every day I laugh life

A non-alcoholic life

Dread head life

Ganja god life

A slides with socks life

A planters life

Reaping the benefits of life

Editing my poetry life

Submitting poems life

Updating my website life

Writing contracts and NDA's life

Paying my child support life

Buying diapers life

 Changing diapers life.

GRACE

In this new place

Silence is the loudest

The cleanliness makes me proudest

We make it to a new section in this rat
race

My dreams are like pb, I have to give
chase

Every meal I eat, I say grace

I got the same phone with the same
case.

FRIDAY'S THERAPY

In Afghan,

I ate bread that began with a B, relaxed

and drank loose leaf tea,

with Sheikhs, I shared meat (currency),

it came with potatoes, no veggies, I

laughed like, "key key", my FENTY

savage like Re Re,

got a queen thicc and brown

like Jay-Z'S, (TGIF) thank God it's friday,

high key.

**TOMORROWS' ANOTHER DAY BUT,
TODAY IS...**

I will too

run away, run away

forever, it can only take an instant

of thinking clever. All of mind

is feeling down to the letter

my headache inflating, like

booties bursting. Inhale on some leaves

my shoulders lift.

tomorrow's another day, but today…

I'm better.

FASTLANE

Memory shot,

thoughts lost in the shuffle,

slow down my mouth

says, yet my feet, weighs heavier

on the pedal. Use to be fiberglass,

now a days all metal old skool,

inside technology new,

behind the wheel experienced driver.

Getting close to eighty miles per hour,

at one hundred shit gets real,

what speed will I breakdown

this time maybe even crash or burn,

every time it happens a lesson I learn.

(like) A Phoenix out of the ashes,

an overpowering energy out of the urn.

Where the fern grows I have not been,

where the dice lands that's how I roll,

safety net NOT 4 ME

I have to tightrope free.

ABOUT THE AUTHOR

Luanie   Lion   BlessUp   Lambey-Bermudez

I am a father of six children (maybe 7, I

have a loose Cock), a husband to a loving, intelligent, beautiful wife. I am a poet at heart who uses different mediums to express that poetry. Twelve years of military service has left me with scars that can and cannot be seen. After a severe mental break, homelessness, and years of being in the care of the VA, I was finally able to get back on my feet. I now live on the Left Coast in Sizzle Town. I am a creator of conversation and promoter of personal growth. Over 10 years as an established poet, writer, serial-expressionist, and magazine editor. I completed bachelor's degree at University of Central Florida and currently enrolled in a master's program at University of Nevada, Las Vegas. BlessUp

NOTES
(THOUGHTS)

TAKE THIS MOMENT TO REFLECT ON
HOW YOU EXPRESS YOUR MENTAL ILL-
NESS. CAN YOUR EXPRESSION RELATE
TO ANY OF THE EXPRESSIONS WRITTEN
ABOVE?